Offerings and Sacrifices of the Old Testament

An Examination of the Old Testament Offerings and Sacrifices and what they Teach us about God and our Relationship with Him

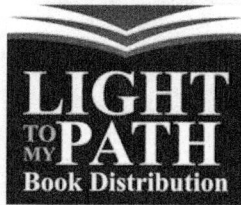

F. Wayne Mac Leod

Light To My Path Book Distribution
Sydney Mines, Nova Scotia, CANADA

Offerings and Sacrifices of the Old Testament

Copyright © 2020 by F. Wayne Mac Leod

Contents

Preface

The Old Testament can be confusing for the new believer. I would venture to say that even the more mature struggle to understand the rituals, sacrifices, and festivals of this time. This study is about the offerings and sacrifices ordained by God in the Law of Moses. Admittedly, this might not be very appealing to the reader, but the reality of the matter is that these sacrifices and offerings have much to teach us about God and the kind of relationship He wants with us.

God gave His law to the Jewish nation, not just to show them how they were to live but also to reveal His nature to them. Through these sacrifices and offerings, the Lord showed His people what was important to Him. He also taught them the seriousness of sin and its implications in their lives. I would venture to say that in these New Testament days, we have often lost sight of what these offerings and sacrifices teach us about God and our responsibility toward Him. As a result, we have become complacent about sin in our lives, our church, and our society.

I trust that as the reader takes the time to examine the teaching in this study, he or she will come to a deeper sense of the holiness of God and His desire for us to walk in that holiness as well. I also trust that it will also give us a greater appreciation of the work the Lord Jesus Christ did on the cross to make forgiveness possible.

May the Lord God be pleased to use this work to elevate His name and bless His people.

F. Wayne Mac Leod

Chapter 1 - The Burnt Offering

The book of Leviticus is the primary source of information about the offerings and sacrifices God expected from His people. Leviticus 1 begins with the law for the burnt offering. Isreal brought this as a tribute to God and recognition of His worth.

From Exodus 29:38-42, we learn that every morning and evening, the priest sacrificed a one-year-old lamb to God.

[38] "Now this is what you shall offer on the altar: two lambs a year old day by day regularly. [39] One lamb you shall offer in the morning, and the other lamb you shall offer at twilight.
[40] And with the first lamb a tenth measure of fine flour mingled with a fourth of a hin of beaten oil, and a fourth of a hin of wine for a drink offering. [41] The other lamb you shall offer at twilight, and shall offer with it a grain offering and its drink offering, as in the morning, for a pleasing aroma, a food offering to the LORD. [42] It shall be a regular burnt offering throughout your generations at the entrance of the tent of meeting before the LORD, where I will meet with you, to speak to you there. (Exodus 29)

On the Sabbath, in addition to the regular morning and evening burnt offerings, the Israelites sacrificed another two one-year-old male lambs to the Lord God as burnt offerings.

[9] "On the Sabbath day, two male lambs a year old without blemish, and two-tenths of an ephah of fine flour for a grain offering, mixed with oil, and its drink offering: [10] this is the

burnt offering of every Sabbath, besides the regular burnt offering and its drink offering. (Numbers 28)

At the beginning of every month, during the new moon, God required two bulls, one ram and seven more lambs for the burnt offering:

[11] At the beginnings of your months, you shall offer a burnt offering to the LORD: two bulls from the herd, one ram, seven male lambs a year old without blemish; [12] also three-tenths of an ephah of fine flour for a grain offering, mixed with oil, for each bull, and two-tenths of fine flour for a grain offering, mixed with oil, for the one ram; [13] and a tenth of fine flour mixed with oil as a grain offering for every lamb; for a burnt offering with a pleasing aroma, a food offering to the LORD. [14] Their drink offerings shall be half a hin of wine for a bull, a third of a hin for a ram, and a quarter of a hin for a lamb. This is the burnt offering of each month throughout the months of the year. (Numbers 28)

The fourteenth day of the first month was the beginning of Passover. At that time, in addition to the regular morning and evening offerings, God expected a burnt offering of seven lambs, two bulls and one ram each day for the seven days of the celebration.

[16] "On the fourteenth day of the first month is the LORD's Passover, [17] and on the fifteenth day of this month is a feast. Seven days shall unleavened bread be eaten. [18] On the first day there shall be a holy convocation. You shall not do any ordinary work, [19] but offer a food offering, a burnt offering to the LORD: two bulls from the herd, one ram, and seven male lambs a year old; see that they are without blemish; ... [23] You

The Burnt Offering
shall offer these besides the burnt offering of the morning,
which is for a regular burnt offering. [24] In the same way you
shall offer daily, for seven days, the food of a food offering,
with a pleasing aroma to the LORD. It shall be offered besides
the regular burnt offering and its drink offering. [25] And on
the seventh day you shall have a holy convocation. You shall
not do any ordinary work. (Numbers 28)

Later, during the celebration of the Feast of Weeks, the priests sacrificed another two bulls, one ram and seven one-year-old lambs:

[26] "On the day of the firstfruits, when you offer a grain
offering of new grain to the LORD at your Feast of Weeks, you
shall have a holy convocation. You shall not do any ordinary
work, [27] but offer a burnt offering, with a pleasing aroma to
the LORD: two bulls from the herd, one ram, seven male lambs
a year old (Numbers 28)

The first day of the seventh month was the celebration of the Feast of Trumpets. Like the other celebrations, this again called for a burnt offering of one bull, one ram and seven one-year-old lambs.

[29:1] "On the first day of the seventh month you shall have a
holy convocation. You shall not do any ordinary work. It is a
day for you to blow the trumpets, [2] and you shall offer a
burnt offering, for a pleasing aroma to the LORD: one bull from
the herd, one ram, seven male lambs a year old without
blemish (Numbers 29)

Ten days after the Feast of Trumpets was the Day of Atonement. Similar to the Feast of Trumpets, Israel again offered one bull, one ram and seven lambs as a burnt offering to the Lord.

[7] "On the tenth day of this seventh month you shall have a holy convocation and afflict yourselves. You shall do no work, [8] but you shall offer a burnt offering to the LORD, a pleasing aroma: one bull from the herd, one ram, seven male lambs a year old: see that they are without blemish. (Numbers 29)

The Feast of Booths on the fifteenth day of the seventh month began with the sacrifice of thirteen bulls, two rams and fourteen lambs. Every day for seven days, the priests sacrificed two rams and fourteen lambs, but the number of bulls required each day decreased by one per day. In total, Israel sacrificed seventy bulls at the Feast of Booths over seven days. On the eighth day, Israel concluded the celebration with the sacrifice of another bull, ram and seven lambs.

God also required burnt offerings at special events in the lives of His children. When a mother purified herself after the birth of a child, she offered a burnt offering to the Lord God. This offering was either a lamb, a turtle dove or a pigeon, depending on what she could afford:

[6] "And when the days of her purifying are completed, whether for a son or for a daughter, she shall bring to the priest at the entrance of the tent of meeting a lamb a year old for a burnt offering, and a pigeon or a turtledove for a sin offering, [7] and he shall offer it before the LORD and make atonement for her. Then she shall be clean from the flow of her blood. This is the law for her who bears a child, either male or female. [8] And if she cannot afford a lamb, then she shall take two turtledoves or two pigeons, one for a burnt offering and

the other for a sin offering. And the priest shall make
atonement for her, and she shall be clean." (Leviticus 12)

God also expected a burnt offering after a person was cleansed from a bodily discharge that defiled him or her. When the individual was cleansed, he or she offered a turtledove or a pigeon to the Lord:

[13] "And when the one with a discharge is cleansed of his
discharge, then he shall count for himself seven days for his
cleansing, and wash his clothes. And he shall bathe his body in
fresh water and shall be clean. [14] And on the eighth day he
shall take two turtledoves or two pigeons and come before the
LORD to the entrance of the tent of meeting and give them to
the priest. [15] And the priest shall use them, one for a sin
offering and the other for a burnt offering. And the priest shall
make atonement for him before the LORD for his discharge.
(Leviticus 15)

If an individual made a special vow to the Lord, upon completion of that vow, he or she offered a male lamb as a burnt offering to the Lord:

[13] "And this is the law for the Nazirite, when the time of his
separation has been completed: he shall be brought to the
entrance of the tent of meeting, [14] and he shall bring his gift
to the LORD, one male lamb a year old without blemish for a
burnt offering, and one ewe lamb a year old without blemish
as a sin offering, and one ram without blemish as a peace
offering, (Numbers 6)

What we see here is that God's people brought burnt offerings every day and during their religious feasts and celebrations. They also brought this offering after they were cleansed from defilement or upon completion of a vow. Along with the burnt offering, the people of Israel generally offered a food offering, drink offering and a sin offering. This fact shows us that the burnt offering was not for cleansing or forgiveness. God also required offerings for forgiveness to be sacrificed alongside the burnt offering. This offering appears to be a tribute paid to God in recognition of His worth and Lordship in the lives of His people.

Leviticus 1 describes the procedure for a burnt offering. Israel brought the offering to the entrance of the tabernacle (Leviticus 1:3). The individuals laid their hands on the head of the animal to remind themselves that it was sacrificed on their behalf (Leviticus 1:4). God expected that the animal offered as a burnt offering be a male without blemish (Leviticus 1:3, 10). After the sacrifice, the priest threw its blood on the sides of the altar (Leviticus 1:5, 11).

If the offering brought was a bull, goat or sheep, the priest would cut it up (Leviticus 1:6, 12) and wash its organs and legs in water (Leviticus 1:9, 13). He would then lay its head and fat on the altar and burn it before the Lord (Leviticus 1:8-9, 13). If the offering was a turtledove or pigeon, the priest would wring off its head (Leviticus 1:14), and drain the blood on the side of the altar (Leviticus 1:15). He would then remove the crop and contents and throw it to the east side of the altar. When that was complete, he tore the bird open by its wings and burnt it on the altar (Leviticus 1:17).

What was unique about the burnt offering is that it was burned in its entirety before the Lord. The whole animal, head, intestines and all were consumed in the fire for the Lord.

What does the offering teach us about God and our relationship with Him?

The question that is important for us in the context of this study is what this sacrifice teaches us about God and our relationship with Him. There are several points I would like to make here about the burnt offering.

Regular Tribute to God

God's people brought the burnt offering twice a day. They also brought additional burnt offerings every month and to each feast or festival in the Old Testament. The burnt offering was a continual reminder to Israel of her indebtedness to the Lord God. When she rose in the morning, she offered her best lambs to her Creator. As the sun went down and she prepared to sleep, she remembered the Lord her God with her unblemished lambs. In every celebration of her nation, she offered her sacrifices to Her Sustainer and Provider.

The burnt offering communicates something significant to us. What place does the remembrance of God have in our daily routine? When we rise in the morning, do we take the time to recognize that He is deserving of our tribute and sacrifice? Do we offer our time, effort and resources to Him as we awake to face the day? Do we end the day with a token of our gratitude to Him for His many blessings?

The burnt offering regularly placed Israel before her God and caused her to remember Him as worthy of all praise and thanksgiving. It forced her to remember that she owed Him much. How easy it is to go through our day without having time for God. How many days have I lived without any recognition of His favour and blessing?

The burnt offering calls us to stop for a moment every day and remember the worthiness and provision of our Creator. As I open my eyes in the morning, I offer myself to Him for His service during the day. As I lay my head down at night, I take a moment to recognize my indebtedness to Him for the blessings of that day. As I lift my spoon to my mouth to nourish my body, I confess God as the source of each benefit I have received. As believers today, we must seek to incorporate times and activities into our lives that keep us in tune with the reality of our need and dependence on the Lord our God. It is easy for us to live our lives without a deep awareness of the source of every blessing.

Recognition of God's Grace in Times of Impurity

God's people offered the burnt offering after being cleansed from impurity. When they recovered from these impurities, they brought a burnt offering to the Lord God.

Consider this for a moment. This impurity caused a separation between God's people and Himself. The holiness of God was such that any defilement, natural or through illness, was an offence to Him. Many things make us unclean before the Lord God. Our thoughts and attitudes can be offensive to Him. Sometimes we don't even intend to think the way we do or say the things we say, but those words and thoughts arise from the flesh within and are an offence to a holy God.

The Burnt Offering

The burnt offering was a reminder to the Israelites that their God was a God of grace. After their cleansing, they offered the Lord a token of their gratitude for His mercy and forgiveness.

There is not a day that goes by that we are not guilty before God of some impurity of thought, action or word. Consider the great patience of God toward us in forgiving and cleansing us of these impurities. As the day comes to a close, recognize that God has been gracious toward you. He has not consumed you in His anger or turned His back on you for your sin. He is deserving of an offering of thanksgiving and praise.

The burnt offering was a symbol of the grace of God in forgiving impurity. It reminded the one who offered his or her sacrifice that God was a patient God who bore with an imperfect and sinful people. It was also a reminder of the seriousness of their impurity. An animal died because of their offence to God. As Israel watched the blood drain from the sacrifice and its body grow limp, they saw just how serious God took their impurity. Their sin and diseases offended God's holiness, but He continued to love them. Our fleshly nature, like a running sore, oozes out its vile attitudes, but God is patient. Just as Israel offered her burnt offering after her cleansing, so we too must take a moment every day to recognize the cleansing work of Christ and offer Him thanksgiving for His wonderful grace and mercy toward us.

Complete Surrender

There is one more detail I want to touch in this chapter. With other offerings, God only required certain parts of the animal to be burnt. The burnt offering, however, was burned completely. The entire animal was consumed on the altar.

There is a lesson for us here. First, we must recognize that this burnt offering points us to the Lord Jesus, who offered Himself entirely for our forgiveness. He held nothing back. He left the glories of heaven. He suffered for His creation and willingly laid down His life for those who rejected Him. He was sacrificed for our forgiveness.

Just as Jesus held nothing back for us, we too must offer ourselves wholly to Him. We must be burnt offerings for Him through the surrender of everything we have. The burnt offering is a symbol of what God requires of us —absolute surrender of all we have and are. As the sun rises in the morning, we lay our lives down before Him as a burnt offering. As the sun sets in the evening, we lay ourselves down to sleep and offer ourselves afresh to Him as a burnt offering, keeping nothing to ourselves. We offer ourselves unconditionally to our Saviour. We do not say, "I am yours as long as it is convenient for me, or I give myself as long as it doesn't cost too much." There were no conditions attached to the burnt offering. God demanded everything.

For Prayer:

Father, the burnt offering reminds us of how much we owe you. You are worthy of our praise and sacrifice. You deserve the daily tribute of our lips and lives. As we rise in the morning, we offer ourselves as a living sacrifice to You. As we lay our heads down at night, we remember your grace and patience with us and offer our token of thanksgiving and praise. Thank you, Lord

The Burnt Offering

Jesus, that you gave Yourself entirely, and without reservation, for our forgiveness. Give us that same attitude. Teach us to take the time each day to recognize what You have done for us. Help us not to become so busy that we fail to confess our indebtedness to You.

Chapter 2 - The Grain Offering

The next Old Testament offering I want to consider is the grain offering. Leviticus 2 describes the requirements for this offering. The grain offering was a mixture of fine flour, oil and frankincense:

> *[2:1] "When anyone brings a grain offering as an offering to the LORD, his offering shall be of fine flour. He shall pour oil on it and put frankincense on it (Leviticus 2)*

While God was clear about the ingredients in the grain offering, the presentation of the offering could differ. An individual could bring the flour mixed with oil and frankincense just as it was. In this case, the priest would take a handful of the mixture and burn it on the altar. This portion given to the Lord was called a memorial portion (Leviticus 2:2). The remainder of the grain offering belonged to the priest and his sons for their personal use (Leviticus 2:3).

The grain offering could also be baked in an oven and made into loaves or wafers. The person bringing the offering was to spread oil on the top of these loaves and presented them to the Lord as a baked grain offering (Leviticus 2:4).

Not everyone would have had access to an oven in those days, so the Lord permitted the worshipper to cook the mixture of flour and oil on a grill. The resulting product was broken into pieces with oil poured over it before bringing it to the priest (Leviticus 2:5-6).

Finally, the worshipper could also cook the grain offering in a pan (Leviticus 2:7). While there was room for a variety of presentations, the essential ingredients were to remain –flour, oil and frankincense. The Lord also permitted the use of salt for these offerings (Leviticus 2:13), but nothing else was to be added or taken away. God prohibited adding yeast or honey to any grain offering.

[11] "No grain offering that you bring to the LORD shall be made with leaven, for you shall burn no leaven nor any honey as a food offering to the LORD.

Leviticus 2:14-16 also permitted the offering of the first fruits of the harvest as a grain offering to the Lord. In this case, the crushed new grain was roasted with fire, sprinkled with oil, and frankincense was laid on top. This crushed, roasted grain would then be brought to the priest. As with the other grain offerings, a memorial portion was burned on the altar, and the remainder belonged to the priest.

One notable exception to the rule was when a priest offered a grain offering on his own behalf. It this case, he was not permitted to keep any of the grain for himself. The entire grain offering was burned on the altar as an offering to the Lord (see Leviticus 6:19-23).

God also required a grain offering alongside the burnt offering. The amount of grain and oil required depended on the animal offered for a burnt offering. Let me provide this chart to simplify God's requirements:

This first chart shows the flour requirements that accompanied a burnt offering with their equivalent in modern

The Grain Offering

measurements. An ephah of flour is estimated to be approximately 17.6 litres or half a bushel.

Animal	Ephah	Litre	UK Gallon	US Gallons
Bull	3/10th	5.28	1.16	1.39
Ram	2/10th	3.52	0.77	0.92
Lamb	1/10th	1.76	0.38	0.45

The oil required for each grain offering was measured in hin. The hin was the equivalent of 3.8 litres. This next chart details and amount of oil that was to accompany the flour per animal.

Animal	Hin	Litre	UK Gallon	US Gallon
Bull	1/2	1.9	0.42	0.50
Ram	1/3	1.26	0.28	0.34
Lamb	¼	0.95	0.21	0.25

According to Leviticus 14, a person cleansed of leprosy was to bring a grain offering to the Lord:

[8] And he who is to be cleansed shall wash his clothes and shave off all his hair and bathe himself in water, and he shall be clean. And after that he may come into the camp, but live outside his tent seven days. [9] And on the seventh day he shall shave off all his hair from his head, his beard, and his eyebrows. He shall shave off all his hair, and then he shall wash his clothes and bathe his body in water, and he shall be clean. [10] "And on the eighth day he shall take two male lambs without blemish, and one ewe lamb a year old without blemish, and a grain offering of three tenths of an ephah of fine flour mixed with oil, and one log of oil. (Leviticus 14)

Also, upon completion of a Nazirite vow, God required another grain offering.

[13] "And this is the law for the Nazirite, when the time of his separation has been completed: he shall be brought to the entrance of the tent of meeting, [14] and he shall bring his gift to the LORD, one male lamb a year old without blemish for a burnt offering, and one ewe lamb a year old without blemish as a sin offering, and one ram without blemish as a peace offering, [15] and a basket of unleavened bread, loaves of fine flour mixed with oil, and unleavened wafers smeared with oil, and their grain offering and their drink offerings. (Numbers 6)

The grain offering was offered alongside the burnt offering as a token of thanksgiving and gratitude to God. It was also brought upon completion of a vow or after healing from an infection. It reminded people of the grace of God and called them to be thankful for His benefits. Because a large portion of the grain offering went to the priest, it was also a way to support the priests and provide for their basic needs.

Let's now take a moment to consider what this offering teaches us about God and His expectations of us as His children.

Variety of Presentation

First, notice that the grain offering was presented to the Lord in a variety of ways. It was brought as it was, cooked in an oven as loaves, cooked on a grill or in a pot. There was room for variety in the offering. The principle is the same today.

Not everybody's offering of praise to God will look the same. As we come to the Lord God with our offering of thanksgiving and praise, my offering will not look the same as my neighbour's. I have a unique personality and express myself to God in a specific way. As we look at believers around us today, we find all kinds of expressions of praise to God. Some churches are lively in their worship. Others are more sedate. Imagine two people coming to the priest with their grain offerings. One offering is baked in an oven while the other was cooked on a grill. What would you think if those two people began to look down on each other because their offering was not prepared in the same way? The grain offerings did not look the same but delighted the Lord. How careful we need to be that we do not criticize our brother or sister because their expression of worship does not look like ours.

No Compromise on the Essential

While there was room for different presentations of the grain offering, there were some essential elements that could never be compromised. God had precise requirements for what went into the grain offering and what was forbidden. Every offering required flour, oil and frankincense. We could speculate as to why these three elements were needed, but that is not our purpose here. What is important is that we understand that all of these ingredients were to be in the grain offering.

God also had a specific recipe for the grain offering. If it was to accompany the burnt offering, then a particular quantity of flour and oil had to be offered. There could be no compromise in these details. An individual could not bring less than what was required, not could they add more.

We learn from this that some things in the worship of God can never be compromised. The challenge for us as the church today is to distinguish between the different presentations of worship and the principles that cannot be compromised. All too often, problems arise in the church because we are not able to make these distinctions.

Believers divide over the style of worship or the type of music used in praise of God. I have met people who have become so focused on the church building that it is more important than God Himself. I have been in churches that focus on particular spiritual gifts and believe that if we are not using these gifts, we are not honouring God. The grain offering teaches us that we need to find a balance between allowing for a variety of presentations in worship without compromising the requirements of God.

No Honey or Yeast

It may be helpful for us to note that the Lord forbade the use of honey or yeast in the grain offerings. Throughout the Scripture, yeast is a symbol of sin. Consider what the apostle Paul wrote to the Corinthians:

[8] Let us therefore celebrate the festival, not with the old leaven, the leaven of malice and evil, but with the unleavened bread of sincerity and truth. (1 Corinthians 5)

Notice how Paul speaks of the leaven of malice and evil. God forbade the use of leaven in the grain offering. We must understand that all our offerings need to be free of sinful attitudes and thoughts. On one occasion, Jesus stood by the offering box in the temple. He watched the rich people come in with their large gifts. He also saw a poor widow bring in the last coins she had. To all outward appearances, the rich gave more, but Jesus saw behind the outward act to the heart of these individuals. He saw the leaven of pride in the hearts of the rich. He saw how they wanted people to see them. The leaven of sin in their hearts made their offerings unacceptable to God. On the other hand, Jesus saw the sacrificial spirit in the poor widow. Her gift touched Him, and it delighted Him more than the large gifts of the rich, given with a self-seeking attitude.

Whatever we do, we must do with a pure heart before God. My offering may not look like the offering of my brother or sister, but if it comes from a genuine and sincere heart, that does not compromise the standard of God, it is acceptable before God.

God also prohibited the use of honey in any grain offering. The sweetness of honey makes our food more attractive. There are many things we can do in an attempt to make our offering or worship of God more appealing.

No doubt, you have heard of churches that do not want to speak about sin because it might offend the newcomer or visitor. In doing so, we water down the gospel. Seminars and courses are offered that teach us how to attract new people and keep them in the church. We do this, however, at the expense of ignoring the Spirit of God and His leading. We become so focused on creating an environment that pleases people that we close our ears to the voice of the Spirit.

Are we not putting honey in our offering to God? Do we believe that the gospel of Jesus and the ministry of the Holy Spirit is enough? Do we feel that we need to make the message more attractive? Do we add to what God has required. The message of the gospel must be kept pure and undefiled by our attempts to make it more appealing. We dare not add honey to the message lest it compromises the truth or water down the message we present.

The offerings we bring may differ one from another, but they must be pure. We must examine every offering we bring to be sure that it is undefiled by the yeast of sin and evil intentions or attitudes. We must also be sure that the honey of compromise is not present in any gift we present to God. We must neither add to nor take away from the requirements of God. Within these parameters, there is the freedom to bring our unique gifts.

Support for God's Workers

There is one final detail we need to understand from the grain offerings. The Lord God required that a large portion of the grain offering go to the priests for their support. The flour, loaves and wafers brought to the temple were a means of providing for the basic needs of the servants of God. These gifts were not financial but very practical. The grain offering provided the priests with bread to eat.

The law of God required that His people provide the practical needs of His priests so that they could devote themselves to full-time service. It is easy for us to assume that the only offerings God accepts today are financial offerings. This, however, is not the case. God's people brought bread and wafers to the temple as an offering. I am part of a church where the women bake or cook a meal and bring it to families in need.

The Grain Offering

This offering is not put in an offering plate at church, but it is a food offering given in the name of the Lord Jesus to His servants. Does not Jesus say:

[42] And whoever gives one of these little ones even a cup of cold water because he is a disciple, truly, I say to you, he will by no means lose his reward." (Matthew 10)

The grain offering shows us that in sharing our food and possessions, we give to the Lord.

For Prayer:

Father, thank you for the lessons we learn from the grain offering of the Old Testament. Thank you that You receive our simple gifts. Teach us to use what You have given us for Your glory. Give us eyes to see the needs around us and hearts that are willing to bless each other. Keep us from judging one another in regard to our worship. Show us what you require, and may we be uncompromisingly faithful. Cause us to examine our lives to be sure that there is no leaven of sin. Keep us from the honey of compromise to make the gospel more appealing.

Chapter 3 - The Drink Offering

In the last chapter, we saw how Israel brought grain offerings (cooked or uncooked) to the priest as a contribution to the Lord. We move now to what was known as the drink offering. The drink offering was an offering of wine. Numbers 28:7 calls this an "offering of strong drink."

[7] Its drink offering shall be a quarter of a hin for each lamb. In the Holy Place you shall pour out a drink offering of strong drink to the LORD. (Numbers 28)

Other Bible versions translate the phrase as "strong wine" (KJV), or "fermented drink" (NIV and NLT). The Hebrew word used here is the word שֵׁכָר šēḵār with is defined as follows in

7941. שֵׁכָר šēḵār: A masculine noun referring to strong drink; beer. It refers to an intoxicating drink and is usually understood as some kind of beer. Priests were not to drink it when serving at the Tabernacle or Temple (Lev 10:9). (Baker, Warren D.R.E., Carpenter, Eugene Ph.D. "7941 שֵׁכָר šēḵār," AMG Word Study Dictionary Old Testament LARIDIAN: Cedar Rapids, Iowa, 2003)

It would appear from this that the wine used was fermented. Note that according to Numbers 10:9, the priests were not permitted to drink this kind of wine when they were on duty:

[8] And the LORD spoke to Aaron, saying, [9] "Drink no wine or strong drink, you or your sons with you, when you go into the

tent of meeting, lest you die. It shall be a statute forever
throughout your generations. (Leviticus 10)

Unlike the grain offering, where the priest offered a memorial portion to the Lord and kept the rest for himself, the drink offering was poured out entirely before the Lord. The priest was not given any of the fermented drink for himself.

Israel's dring offering usually accompanied other offerings. The amount of wine required for the offering depended on the animal sacrificed at the time. Numbers 15:4-10 details the requirements of God.

Animal	Hin	Litre	Gallon (UK)	Gallon (US)
Bull	½	1.9	0.42	0.50
Ram	1/3	1.26	0.28	0.34
Lamb	¼	0.95	0.21	0.25

Numbers 15:4 tells us that the drink offering was a "pleasing aroma to the LORD:"

[7] And for the drink offering you shall offer a third of a hin of
wine, a pleasing aroma to the LORD. (Numbers 15)

The drink offering was brought to the Lord after the completion of a Nazirite vow. At that time, the individual completing his vow brought this along with his burnt offering.

[13] "And this is the law for the Nazirite, when the time of his
separation has been completed: he shall be brought to the
entrance of the tent of meeting, [14] and he shall bring his gift
to the LORD, one male lamb a year old without blemish for a
burnt offering, and one ewe lamb a year old without blemish
as a sin offering, and one ram without blemish as a peace

offering, [15] and a basket of unleavened bread, loaves of fine flour mixed with oil, and unleavened wafers smeared with oil, and their grain offering and their drink offerings. [16] And the priest shall bring them before the LORD and offer his sin offering and his burnt offering, [17] and he shall offer the ram as a sacrifice of peace offering to the LORD, with the basket of unleavened bread. The priest shall offer also its grain offering and its drink offering. (Numbers 6)

Genesis 35:9-15 describes how God met Jacob in the region of Paddan-Aram. On that occasion, the Lord blessed Jacob and changed his name to Israel, promising to make his descendants a great nation. When the Lord left, Jacob set up a pillar and poured out a drink offering on it:

[14] And Jacob set up a pillar in the place where he had spoken with him, a pillar of stone. He poured out a drink offering on it and poured oil on it. [15] So Jacob called the name of the place where God had spoken with him Bethel. (Genesis 35)

In this instance, we have no record of an associated animal sacrifice. Jacob poured out his drink offering and, according to Genesis 35:14, added some oil to it. He gave this offering to the Lord in response to His wonderful promises to make his descendants into a great nation. It was a token of thanksgiving and gratitude to God.

On two separate occasions, the apostle Paul used the illustration of the drink offering to speak of his own life and ministry. In Philippians 2, the apostle wrote to the Philippians about his hard work on their behalf:

[16] holding fast to the word of life, so that in the day of Christ I may be proud that I did not run in vain or labor in vain. [17]

31

Offerings and Sacrifices of the Old Testament
Even if I am to be poured out as a drink offering upon the
sacrificial offering of your faith, I am glad and rejoice with you
all. (Philippians 2)

Paul uses the words "run," "labour," and "sacrificial offering" to describe the effort he had made for the believers in Philippi. He challenged the believers to hold fast to the word of life he had taught them so that these labours would not be in vain. Paul told the Philippians that if he were poured out as a drink offering, it would be upon the faith of the Philippians. This phrase merits some consideration.

The drink offering was often poured out on an accompanying offering. The offering Paul speaks about here is the faith of the Philippians. Through the apostle's ministry, many Philippians had come to faith in Jesus Christ. Paul was pleased to offer these converts to the Lord as the fruit of his hard labours. This was a gift in which God was well-pleased for nothing delights Him more than that the lost come to know His Son.

Paul told the Philippians that if he had to die for this work, his death would be like a drink offering poured out on their faith. He poured out his life as a drink offering on the new-found faith of the Philippians. Just as God would be pleased with the faith of the Philippians, so He would be pleased with the efforts of Paul, poured out on them.

In Timothy 4, as the apostle comes to the end of his life, he said to Timothy:

[6] For I am already being poured out as a drink offering, and
the time of my departure has come. [7] I have fought the good
fight, I have finished the race, I have kept the faith. [8]
Henceforth there is laid up for me the crown of righteousness,

The Drink Offering

which the Lord, the righteous judge, will award to me on that day, and not only to me but also to all who have loved His appearing. (2 Timothy 4)

Paul compared his life to a drink offering poured out entirely for the Lord God. He had fought a good fight. He had finished the race. He had kept the faith. He knew that he had given his all for the cause of the Lord.

What should we learn from the drink offering? There are two points I want to make here.

Poured Out Completely

The apostle Paul saw his life as a drink offering poured out entirely for the Lord. This is how Paul looked at his life. His attitude is in direct contrast to the teaching that all believers should prosper materially in this world. Material blessings were not the focus of Paul's life, nor were they the focus of Jesus. Listen to the Lord's words in Matthew 8:

[20] And Jesus said to him, "Foxes have holes, and birds of the air have nests, but the Son of Man has nowhere to lay his head." (Matthew 8)

Jesus devoted His life to the will of the Father. He did not have a home or even a bed to lay on at night. His entire life was given to accomplish the purpose of the Father. He held nothing back but gave Himself for our salvation. He sets an example for us to follow.

What does it mean for you to follow the Lord Jesus today? Do you follow Him like the people of His day –for what you can get out of Him? Or are you willing to pour out your life like a drink offering? We certainly are to delight in the good things God gives. The Christian life is a life of receiving from God, for we cannot give unless we receive from Him. We are not to grow fat on those blessings, however, but share them with those around us. We are to use what He gives and pour out his resources on those God sends our way.

Paul willingly suffered for the Lord and His cause. He was mocked, beaten and stoned for the gospel he represented. He was imprisoned for relentlessly preaching the good news of Jesus.

Is your life a drink offering to the Lord? Are you a channel of refreshing through which the Spirit of God can flow, or is that stream blocked? Will you submit yourself to the Spirit of God today for Him to use as He sees fit. Will you pour out your strength and efforts for the cause of the Father?

Pleasing Aroma to God

The drink offering is described as a pleasing aroma to God. That wine poured out on the sacrificed animal, pleased the Lord and delighted His heart. Consider the fact that we have all fallen short of the standard of God. Consider the attitudes of our heart and the weakness of our efforts. How could our efforts ever please the Lord God?

Some years ago, I was refinishing the stairs in my house. My grandson was living with us at the time. He watched me work, scraping and sanding the wood on the steps. On one occasion, he climbed up the steps and stood with me. Picking up a scraper, he began to imitate what he had seen me do. He was not strong enough to apply the pressure required to scrap off the old paint and varnish, and I had to put my work aside to keep him from falling down the stairs. I remember this occasion fondly, however. His imitation of my efforts was a delight to my heart. The fact that he wanted to help me was a tremendous blessing.

Somehow, as feeble as I am in my efforts for God, He is still pleased. My sincere efforts to obey and walk in obedience to Him, delight His heart. As I offer myself, all these efforts rise up to Him as a pleasing aroma. This is my act of worship.

Listen to the words of Paul to the Romans:

[12:1] I appeal to you therefore, brothers, by the mercies of God, to present your bodies as a living sacrifice, holy and acceptable to God, which is your spiritual worship. (Romans 12)

Notice that Paul told the Romans that they were to present their bodies as a living sacrifice. This offering was a holy and acceptable offering to God. God delighted in their sacrifice. It rose to Him as a sweet-smelling fragrance. How do we please God? We do so by pouring out our lives as a drink offering to the Lord entirely and without reserve. This kind of sacrifice is a blessing to His heart and a sweet aroma in His nostrils.

For Prayer:

Father, I ask that my life would be poured out to you, just like the Old Testament drink offering. I pray that I would hold nothing back but devote myself entirely to you. Forgive me for making my life about all that I can receive and teach me what you mean when you say that it was more blessed to give than to receive. I pray that I would live my life so that when I come to stand before you, I would have the confidence to say, I have fought a good fight, I have run a good race, I have kept the faith. My life has been a drink offering and a pleasing aroma to you.

Chapter 4 - The Peace Offering

Leviticus 3 explains the requirements of God for the peace offering. The animal offered was an unblemished male or female either from a herd or flock. Individuals bringing their gift would lay their hands on the head of the animal and kill it at the front of the tabernacle. The priest would take the blood and throw it against the altar. The fat, the kidneys and the long lobe of the liver were removed and burned as an offering to the Lord on the altar (see Leviticus 3:3-5; 7-11; 12-16).

Leviticus 7:11-18 tells us that an individual could bring a peace offering out of thankfulness to God (verses 11-15) or as part of a vow he or she had made (verses 16-18). An offering of unleavened loaves or wafers made with fine flour and oil accompanied the peace offering (Leviticus 7:12).

One of the loaves brought with the peace offering belonged to the priest who performed the sacrifice (Leviticus 7:15). Leviticus 7:32 tells us that the right thigh (Leviticus 7:32-33) and the breast (Leviticus 7:34) also belonged to the priest as a contribution from the worshipper. The remainder of the animal was returned to the individual who brought it. The worshipper would eat the meat with "rejoicing before the Lord." Eating this meat and rejoicing before the Lord was an essential part of the offering.

[17] You may not eat within your towns the tithe of your grain or of your wine or of your oil, or the firstborn of your herd or of

your flock, or any of your vow offerings that you vow, or your freewill offerings or the contribution that you present, [18] but you shall eat them before the LORD your God in the place that the LORD your God will choose, you and your son and your daughter, your male servant and your female servant, and the Levite who is within your towns. And you shall rejoice before the LORD your God in all that you undertake. [19] Take care that you do not neglect the Levite as long as you live in your land. (Deuteronomy 12)

The meat of the peace offering was eaten on the day of the offering –nothing was to be left over until the morning.

[15] And the flesh of the sacrifice of his peace offerings for thanksgiving shall be eaten on the day of his offering. He shall not leave any of it until the morning. (Leviticus 7)

The only exception to this rule was if the peace offering was given as a result of a vow. In this case, the individual could eat the meat the day after the sacrifice. Anything left over on the third day, however, was to be burned:

[16] But if the sacrifice of his offering is a vow offering or a freewill offering, it shall be eaten on the day that he offers his sacrifice, and on the next day what remains of it shall be eaten. [17] But what remains of the flesh of the sacrifice on the third day shall be burned up with fire. (Leviticus 7)

To eat the meat of the peace offering after the second day would invalidate the sacrifice and make the individual guilty of sin:

[18] If any of the flesh of the sacrifice of his peace offering is eaten on the third day, he who offers it shall not be accepted,

The Peace Offering

neither shall it be credited to him. It is tainted, and he who eats of it shall bear his iniquity. (Leviticus 7)

Israel brought peace offerings to the Lord on a variety of occasions. It was part of the celebration of the Feast of Weeks (Leviticus 23:15-19). Upon completion of a Nazirite vow, the Israelite would offer a peace offering to the Lord (Numbers 6:16-20). A peace offering was also one of the sacrifices required for the consecration of a priest to his position (Exodus 29:19-28).

One of the largest peace offerings recorded in Scripture took place at the dedication of Solomon's temple. At that time, King Solomon offered 22,000 oxen and 120,000 sheep:

[62] Then the king, and all Israel with him, offered sacrifice before the LORD. [63] Solomon offered as peace offerings to the LORD 22,000 oxen and 120,000 sheep. So the king and all the people of Israel dedicated the house of the LORD. (1 Kings 8)

1 Samuel 11 describes the trouble Israel had with the Ammonites. Led by the Lord, Saul took up arms and defeated them at Bezek. After the battle, 1 Samuel 11:12-15 tells us that Samuel led them in the sacrifice of a peace offering in gratitude to God for the victory.

2 Chronicles 29:31-36 describes a time of renewal when the temple was purified of its impurities. Part of the consecration of the people in those days involved a peace offering.

While there were certain times of the year when God required a peace offering, it was also offered voluntarily on special occasions as an act of worship and thanksgiving to God.

A Sacrifice of Gratitude

There are several details about the peace offering we need to examine more closely. Notice first that while God required a peace offering on certain occasions, it was also a voluntary sacrifice brought out of gratitude. Consider this for a moment. When God gave Israel victory over her oppressors in 1 Samuel 11, the people expressed their appreciation by bringing a peace offering. When the temple was cleansed after years of abandonment, the people of God repented and brought their voluntary peace offering. This peace offering went further than a simple "thank you" to God. In response to His goodness, the people sacrificed a lamb from the flock to celebrate God's goodness. They shared that lamb with the priest and their family as they ate together in gratitude.

What is our response when we know the victory of the Lord after a long battle? What is our reaction when we experience forgiveness from our sin and rebellion? Somehow a simple "thanks" does not seem to be enough. The deliverance of the Lord demands a sacrifice of our lives, resources and energies. The peace offering was not just a sacrifice, however, it was also a celebration and sharing the goodness of God with others. A portion of the sacrifice blessed the priest. The family ate the meat of this sacrifice in celebration of the goodness and deliverance of God. God's people remembered His kindness and shared their blessing with others. When God brings deliverance and victory, this is a cause for celebration. May God give us the grace to know how to express our gratitude in deeper ways.

The Peace Offering

Honouring God in our Sacrifices

Another significant point we need to see in the law of the peace offering is that while the sacrifice was voluntary and God allowed for freedom in what His people could bring, it still had to be without blemish. God deserved the very best they had. They could not give Him what they did not want themselves and expect that He would be pleased.

When God stopped the plague on the nation because of the sin of David, the king chose to offer a peace offering to Him. He asked a man by the name of Araunah to sell him a piece of property on which he could offer his sacrifice. Araunah offered to give the property to David without cost. Listen to the response of David to this offer in 2 Samuel 24:

> *[24] But the king said to Araunah, "No, but I will buy it from you for a price. I will not offer burnt offerings to the LORD my God that cost me nothing." So David bought the threshing floor and the oxen for fifty shekels of silver. [25] And David built there an altar to the LORD and offered burnt offerings and peace offerings. So the LORD responded to the plea for the land, and the plague was averted from Israel. (2 Samuel 24)*

After all that God had done for him, David refused to offer a sacrifice that cost him nothing. David wanted His act of worship to involve personal sacrifice. He gave the best he had. Are we giving God what cost us nothing? Are we giving what we do not want or need ourselves? Or are we giving the best we have? What do our offerings tell us about what we feel about God? What sacrifices are you willing to make for God as a result of His blessings in your life?

Notice that nothing of the peace offering was left over until the morning. The greatest offering of all time was the Lord Jesus as the Lamb of God. He hung on a cross to pay the legal penalty for our sin. This penalty gives us peace with God. Consider what took place when the Lord Jesus died as recorded in Mark 15:

[42] And when evening had come, since it was the day of Preparation, that is, the day before the Sabbath, [43] Joseph of Arimathea, a respected member of the council, who was also himself looking for the kingdom of God, took courage and went to Pilate and asked for the body of Jesus. [44] Pilate was surprised to hear that he should have already died. And summoning the centurion, he asked him whether he was already dead. [45] And when he learned from the centurion that he was dead, he granted the corpse to Joseph. (Mark 15)

It was the evening of the death of Jesus that His body was taken down from the cross and buried. It was not left hanging there until the next day. While there were health reasons why the meat of the peace offering could not be left over until the next day, there is also a symbolism found in this requirement as well. It points us to the most excellent peace offering ever made and how the Lamb of God was not left on the cross until the next day.

Notice something else about the peace offering. The meat remaining after the Lord and the priest had received their portion was eaten with the family. Israel did this in remembrance of the goodness of God. Consider the words of the Lord Jesus in Matthew 26 when He instituted the Lord's Supper:

The Peace Offering

[26] Now as they were eating, Jesus took bread, and after blessing it broke it and gave it to the disciples, and said, "Take, eat; this is my body." [27] And he took a cup, and when he had given thanks he gave it to them, saying, "Drink of it, all of you, [28] for this is my blood of the covenant, which is poured out for many for the forgiveness of sins. [29] I tell you I will not drink again of this fruit of the vine until that day when I drink it new with you in my Father's kingdom." (Matthew 26)

Jesus asked His disciples to share a meal in remembrance of the sacrifice He would make on the cross. They took bread and drank wine to symbolize the broken body and blood spilled for them. As a family of believers, they shared a meal to celebrate their victory. This is what took place with the peace offering.

God's people brought a peace offering in response to the goodness of God. They shared the meat of the animal sacrificed with the priest, and the members of their family. They ate together, celebrating the goodness of God. Certainly as believers, we have cause for rejoicing. Eating the peace offering together provided God's people with the opportunity to remember and share the goodness of their God.

For Prayer:

Father, we recognize that you have blessed us abundantly in this life. As we look over our lives, we are aware of the tremendous victories you have given us time and time again. Somehow a simple "thank you" does not seem sufficient for these blessings. We pray that you would teach us to give our sacrifices to you in return. We offer our lives, our efforts, our resources to you, realizing that these cannot compare to what you have done for us. Teach us to bring the best we have to you. Forgive us for offering sacrifices that cost us nothing. We thank you also for the greatest peace offering of all time—the sacrifice of the Lord Jesus on the cross of Calvary. Teach us to be thankful for His life and death. Give us the grace to become living sacrifices for Him. Father, teach us not to keep our blessing to ourselves. Help us to share the goodness of God. May we be a celebrating people who declare to our family and those around us the goodness of God.

Chapter 5 - The Sin Offering

The next offering recorded in the book of Leviticus is the sin offering. Notice the words of introduction in Leviticus 4:2:

[2] "Speak to the people of Israel, saying, If anyone sins unintentionally in any of the LORD's commandments about things not to be done, and does any one of them,

This verse shows us the purpose of the sin offering – "if anyone sins unintentionally in any of the Lord's commandments." Jamieson, Fausset and Brown, in their commentary on this verse, say the following:

"The sins, however, referred to in this law were unintentional violations of the ceremonial laws, —breaches made through haste, or inadvertency of some negative precepts, which, if done knowingly and wilfully, would have involved a capital punishment." (Jamieson, Robert; Fausset, A.R.; Brown, David: Commentary Critical and Explanatory on the Whole Bible, "Leviticus 4:2" LARIDIAN, 1871)

The sin offering involved an animal sacrifice for sins done unintentionally. This offering was not for those who willfully sinned against the Lord. Consider what the Lord Jesus said about those who crucified Him in Luke 23:

[34] And Jesus said, "Father, forgive them, for they know not what they do." And they cast lots to divide his garments. (Luke 23)

Notice that Jesus prayed for the forgiveness of those who did not know what they did. These individuals acted in ignorance because they did not truly understand the truth about Jesus. There is hope for those who have not come to the knowledge of the truth.

Writing to Timothy, the apostle Paul said

[12] I thank him who has given me strength, Christ Jesus our Lord, because he judged me faithful, appointing me to his service, [13] though formerly I was a blasphemer, persecutor, and insolent opponent. But I received mercy because I had acted ignorantly in unbelief, [14] and the grace of our Lord overflowed for me with the faith and love that are in Christ Jesus. (1 Timothy 1)

At one point in the apostle's life, he was a great enemy to the church of Jesus Christ. He actively persecuted believers and rejected the Lord Jesus as the Son of God. Paul told Timothy, however, that through he was a blasphemer, persecutor and insolent opponent to the gospel, he received mercy because he "acted ignorantly in unbelief." At this time, the apostle had not come to an understanding of the truth of Jesus. He persecuted the church because he had never met the Lord. Everything changed the day he came to know Him.

While there is forgiveness for sins done in unbelief and ignorance, the writer to the Hebrews warns us that deliberate and willful sin is a different matter:

[26] For if we go on sinning deliberately after receiving the knowledge of the truth, there no longer remains a sacrifice for sins, [27] but a fearful expectation of judgment, and a fury of fire that will consume the adversaries. (Hebrews 10)

The Sin Offering

There is no sacrifice for those who deliberately turn their back on the Lord Jesus after coming to know the truth about Him. The writer to the Hebrews tells us that the only hope for those who willfully reject the truth is a "fearful expectation of judgment and a fury of fire." The sin offering was not intended for those who deliberately sinned but those who sinned through ignorance or weakness.

The animal sacrificed for the sin offering depended on the social status of the individual bringing the offering. The following chart explains the requirements of God for each social status in the community:

Individual	Offering	Passage
Priest	Young bull	Leviticus 4:3
Congregation	Young bull	Leviticus 4:13-14
Leader	Male goat	Leviticus 4:22-23
Common People	Female goat or lamb	Leviticus 4:27-32
Poor person	2 turtledoves or pigeons OR 1/10th ephah of flour	Leviticus 5:7 Leviticus 5:11

God required the following for a priest who unintentionally sinned against Him:

1) The guilty priest brought his offering to the entrance of the tabernacle (Lev. 4:4)
2) He laid his hand on the animal to identify with its demise
3) They killed the animal at the entrance (Leviticus 4:4)

4) The officiating priest took the blood into the tabernacle and sprinkled it seven times in front of the curtain before the Holy of Holies (Leviticus 4:5)

5) The officiating priest put blood on the horns of the altar and poured the remainder at the base of the altar (Leviticus 4:7)

6) The officiating priest removed the fat, the two kidneys and the long lobe of the liver from the animal and burned them on the altar as an offering to the Lord (Leviticus 4:8-10)

7) The remainder of the animal was carried outside the camp and burned (Leviticus 4:11-12)

The priests followed the same procedure when the whole community was guilty. If the offering was for a leader or ordinary person, the priest did not sprinkle blood in front of the curtain in the tabernacle. All other steps, however, were the same.

When a poor person brought a bird as an offering for sin, the priest would follow this procedure:

1) The guilty party brought his or her offering of two pigeons or turtledoves to the priest (Leviticus 5:8)

2) The priest wrung the neck of the bird to kill it (Leviticus 5:8)

3) The priest sprinkled blood on the side of the altar and the remainder at the base (Leviticus 5:9)

4) The priest burned the second bird on the altar (Leviticus 5:10)

If the poor person could not afford two pigeons or turtledoves, he or she would bring $1/10^{th}$ of an ephah of fine flour. There was to be no oil or frankincense in the flour. The priest took a handful of this flour and burned it on the altar as a sin offering. The promise of God for those who brought these offerings was that they would be forgiven:

[13] Thus the priest shall make atonement for him for the sin which he has committed in any one of these things, and he shall be forgiven. (Leviticus 5)

God required that Israel offer Him a sin-offering during their yearly festivals and celebrations:

Celebration	Passage
New Moon	Numbers 28:15
Passover	Numbers 28:22
Feast of Weeks	Numbers 28:30
Feast of Trumpets	Numbers 29:5
Day of Atonement	Numbers 29:11
Feast of Booths	Numbers 29: 16,19,22,25,28,31,34,38

Besides these regular celebrations, God required a sin offering as part of the purification rite after recovering from childbirth, infection or disease (see Leviticus 12:6-8; Leviticus 14:19; 15:13-15). It was also required when a Nazirite vow had to be broken for unforeseen reasons (see Numbers 6:1-11).

Leviticus 5 gives us further examples of occasions when a sin offering was required.

1) When a witness to a crime or offence did not speak up about what he or she saw (Leviticus 5:1)
2) When a person touched a dead body, an unclean animal, insect, or human impurity (Leviticus 5:2,3)

3) When a person uttered a careless or thoughtless oath (Leviticus 5:4)

The sin offering was not just for obvious sins but also for sins of omission —when an individual did not do what he or she was supposed to do. It covered careless words spoken by the people of God, as well as things they saw and touched that defiled them.

The sin offering was vital in the life of Israel. It offered forgiveness for sin. For this reason, the meat of the sin offering was considered holy.

[25] "Speak to Aaron and his sons, saying, This is the law of the sin offering. In the place where the burnt offering is killed shall the sin offering be killed before the LORD; it is most holy.
(Leviticus 6)

Because this offering was holy, there were special restrictions placed on it. Leviticus 6 tells us that only the priest who offered it to the Lord could eat it, but only in the tabernacle. It was not eaten anywhere else:

[26] The priest who offers it for sin shall eat it. In a holy place it shall be eaten, in the court of the tent of meeting. (Leviticus 6)

This sacrifice was so holy that if it touched anything, the object it touched become holy – "Whatever touches its flesh shall be holy" (Leviticus 6:27). If the blood of this sacrifice splashed on a garment, it was only to be washed off in a holy place. (Leviticus 6:27).

If the priest cooked the meat offered for a sin offering in an earthenware vessel, the vessel was broken and discarded. It was never used to cook anything else (Leviticus 6:28). If the container used for preparing the holy meat was bronze, it was thoroughly cleaned with water before being used again (Leviticus 6:28). The sin offering was treated with the utmost respect.

What do we learn from the sin offering about God and our relationship with Him? Let me offer several suggestions.

The Seriousness of Deliberate Sin

Consider first that the sin offering was for unintentional sins. There was no offering for deliberate and intentional sin. The judgement of God fell on all who, knowing the truth, refuse it and reject God's purpose for their lives. Hell and eternal punishment is the only reward left for those who deliberately turn from the truth they know. As the apostle Peter says:

[20] For if, after they have escaped the defilements of the world through the knowledge of our Lord and Savior Jesus Christ, they are again entangled in them and overcome, the last state has become worse for them than the first. [21] For it would have been better for them never to have known the way of righteousness than after knowing it to turn back from the holy commandment delivered to them. (2 Peter 2)

God Recognizes our Imperfections

God expects that those who belonged to Him serve Him with all their heart. He understands, however, that we are not perfect. We all have our weaknesses. The Lord knows that not one of us will live a perfect life. We will fall short of His standard, I fall into temptation and sin against him. We will sin because of human weakness.

All sin needs forgiveness. It is easy to excuse our actions. None of those excuses are valid. Yes, we are weak. Yes, it was only natural for us to respond as we do. But we still fall short of God's standard, and God holds us responsible for our actions.

God knows our imperfections, but we tend to use them as an excuse to justify our sin instead of seeking His forgiveness. God has provided a means for cleansing due to human weakness and failure. The fact that the sin offering was established for sins committed through weakness and failures shows us that none of our excuses are legitimate. Our inability to keep God's standard through human weakness requires forgiveness. God provided Israel with a means of forgiveness for these unintentional sins in the sin offering.

God's Forgiveness is for Everyone

Notice that the sin offering was for everyone in society. If a poor person could not afford a lamb, they could bring a turtledove or pigeon. If they did not have the money to purchase these birds, they could bring flour. This provision of God shows us just how important it was for people of all status in society to experience the forgiveness of God.

God wanted to forgive the wealthy and influential, but He was also concerned for those who were at the bottom of the social ladder. There was forgiveness for everyone, regardless of social standing. Jesus demonstrated this in His ministry on earth. Those whom the religious leaders rejected found hope and forgiveness in the Lord Jesus. The tax collectors and sinners knew His pardon as did those in positions of respect and honour. The sin offering was for all.

Responsibility of Those in Authority

While the sin offering was for all. Notice that the Lord required a bull as a sin offering from the priest, a ram from a community leader, a lamb from the ordinary person and flour from the poorest and most uneducated. This difference should not go unnoticed. Consider the words of Jesus in Luke 12:

[48] But the one who did not know, and did what deserved a beating, will receive a light beating. Everyone to whom much was given, of him much will be required, and from him to whom they entrusted much, they will demand the more. (Luke 12)

God has a higher expectation of those who have been given greater responsibility. If you are a pastor and leader of His people, you have a greater responsibility to be an example for the flock. Your sin will have a more significant impact on the testimony of the church. Listen to the words of James

[3:1] Not many of you should become teachers, my brothers, for you know that we who teach will be judged with greater strictness. (James 3)

Positions of authority come with their obligations and responsibilities. God requires more of those to whom He has given these greater obligations and responsibilities.

Take all Sin Seriously

Another important lesson from the sin offering comes from Leviticus 6. This passage tells us that God required a sin offering for things Israel did not do as well as those things she did. If a person witnessed a crime and said nothing about it, he or she was guilty before God and needed to offer a sin offering for what they did not say.

If a person spoke something without thinking, they were also guilty. For example, if he or she said they would do something but never got around to it, they needed to confess this to God. If, in the anger of the moment, they spoke harshly and thoughtlessly to a brother or sister, they needed to acknowledge this and make things right again.

If an individual touched something impure without knowing it, when it was revealed to them, they were to confess this and come to God for forgiveness. How many times do we use the excuse, "I didn't know?" Ignorance is not an excuse for sin. You don't have to know you have sinned to be guilty. You don't have to intentionally sin to be accountable for your actions. When you are made aware of your failure, however, you need to confess this to God without seeking to excuse yourself.

Impurities come in many different forms. In the Old Testament, a person might touch the corpse of an unclean insect during their daily routine. This would not have been intentional, but it still made them impure. Consider the impurities that defile our minds through the things we unintentionally see and hear in a day. Like the people of the Old Testament, these impurities fill our minds and hearts with impure thoughts and attitudes. These things defile our hearts and mind. God has made provision for us to come to Him for the cleansing of these impurities. We must not let them remain but seek Him for deliverance. This will often require going to God for help and victory.

The Holiness of the Offering

Let me conclude with a final thought about the holiness of the sin offering. The law of God required that the sin offering be treated with the utmost respect and dignity. It was eaten in a holy place. Anything this offering touched would become holy. There is a reason for this. The sin offering brought forgiveness and restored the relationship between God and His people.

Sin separated God from His people. Without the forgiveness of sin, there could be no hope for the people of God. Hell and eternal separation is the reality for those who refuse this offer of God. The sin offering was a picture of the Lord Jesus who laid down His life so that we could be pardoned and restored to a right relationship with God.

The work of Jesus for us on the cross is one we must take very seriously. It is our hope and confidence. Apart from His work, there is no hope of forgiveness. The Lord Jesus, as a sin offering, must never be despised or treated with contempt. He must be lifted high and honoured with all that we have for apart from Him, we would be eternally lost.

For Prayer:

Lord God, I want to thank you for the provision you made for sin. Thank you that the Lord Jesus came to be a sin offering for us so that we could be pardoned and restored to a relationship with you. Father, forgive us for excusing our sin. Teach us to bring all our shortcomings and failures to you for forgiveness. Cleanse us from sins we are not currently aware of. Cleanse our hearts and minds of the defilements of this world, its lusts and temptations. Help us to always honour the work of the Lord Jesus for our forgiveness. Thank you that while we often fall short of your standard, You have, in your mercy, made a provision for the cleansing of all our weaknesses and shortcomings through Jesus, Your Son.

Chapter 6 - The Guilt Offering

In Leviticus 5:14-6:7 the Lord explains the reason and requirements for the guilt offering. Israel brought a guilt offering when their actions caused a brother or sister to suffer loss. The guilt offering differed from the sin offering in that the individual who brought the offering also need make restitution to the individual he or she had offended. Israel brought this type of offering for breaches of faith toward God or a fellow citizen.

Consider first a breach of faith toward God. Leviticus 5:15 tells us that God required a guilt offering from anyone who sinned unintentionally "in any of the holy things of the Lord:

[15] "If anyone commits a breach of faith and sins unintentionally in any of the holy things of the LORD, he shall bring to the LORD as his compensation, a ram without blemish out of the flock, valued in silver shekels, according to the shekel of the sanctuary, for a guilt offering. (Leviticus 5)

We have an example of this in Leviticus 22:

[14] And if anyone eats of a holy thing unintentionally, he shall add the fifth of its value to it and give the holy thing to the priest. (Leviticus 22)

It might be possible for someone to eat meat, not knowing that it was dedicated to the Lord. When this happened, the law of God required that the person who had sinned in this manner make restitution for what he had eaten, add one fifth to it and give it to the priest. He was also to sacrifice a ram as a guilt offering for his offence:

> *[16] He shall also make restitution for what he has done amiss in the holy thing and shall add a fifth to it and give it to the priest. And the priest shall make atonement for him with the ram of the guilt offering, and he shall be forgiven. (Leviticus 5)*

Another example of a breach of faith before God was in the case of a Nazirite vow. Isreal placed themselves under such a vow for various reasons. The individual engaged in such a commitment refused to drink wine or strong drink, cut their hair or touch a dead body until their oath was fulfilled (Numbers 6:1-8).

Numbers 6:9 describes a situation where a man died suddenly beside an individual taking a Nazirite vow. The body of this dead man touched the individual under the vow, breaking His commitment to God:

> *[9] "And if any man dies very suddenly beside him and he defiles his consecrated head, then he shall shave his head on the day of his cleansing; on the seventh day he shall shave it.*
> *(Numbers 6)*

Because he touched the body of a dead person, he unintentionally broke his commitment to God, through no fault of his own. This required that the individual making the vow go into isolation for seven days. On the eighth day, he was to bring a guilt offering (Numbers 6:12) to the Lord before recommencing the time of his vow.

The Guilt Offering

What was true of offences toward God was also true of offences toward a fellow citizen. God required a guilt offering anytime there was a breach of faith between two parties. Leviticus 6 gives us some examples.

1) If an individual deceived his neighbour regarding something held in security (6:2)
2) If an individual robbed another (6:2)
3) If an individual oppressed his or her neighbour in some way (6:2)
4) If an individual found something that belonged to another and lied about it (6:3)

When the deception was discovered, the guilty party was to restore what he or she had taken and added one-fifth of the value to it. He also brought a ram to the priest as a guilt offering (Leviticus 6:6). Only then would his or her sin be forgiven.

Leviticus 19:20-22 describes another situation where a guilt offering was required:

[20] "If a man lies sexually with a woman who is a slave, assigned to another man and not yet ransomed or given her freedom, a distinction shall be made. They shall not be put to death, because she was not free; [21] but he shall bring his compensation to the LORD, to the entrance of the tent of meeting, a ram for a guilt offering. [22] And the priest shall make atonement for him with the ram of the guilt offering before the LORD for his sin that he has committed, and he shall be forgiven for the sin that he has committed. (Leviticus 19)

In this case, the slave girl belonged to another person. The man who slept with her violated what belonged to her master.

Leviticus 7 details the procedure for offering a guilt offering:

1) The guilty party brought his or her offering to the tabernacle (vs. 2)
2) The sacrifice was killed at the tabernacle (vs. 2)
3) The priest took the blood of the offering and throw it against the sides of the altar (vs. 2)
4) The fat, the two kidneys and the lobe of the liver were removed and burned on the altar (vs. 3)
5) The skin and the meat belonged to the priest for his use (vs. 6-8)

A vital component of the guilt offering was the restitution of what an individual lost. While this restitution was generally made to the offended party, in some cases, that individual was no longer alive. The death of the offended party did not excuse the guilty person. Restitution was made in this case to the next of kin.

[6] "Speak to the people of Israel, When a man or woman commits any of the sins that people commit by breaking faith with the LORD, and that person realizes his guilt, [7] he shall confess his sin that he has committed. And he shall make full restitution for his wrong, adding a fifth to it and giving it to him to whom he did the wrong. [8] But if the man has no next of kin to whom restitution may be made for the wrong, the restitution for wrong shall go to the LORD for the priest, in addition to the ram of atonement with which atonement is made for him. (Numbers 5)

The guilty party was not relieved of his accountability at the death of the offended person. Sin still had to be atoned for, and the family recompensed for what had been taken from them.

The Guilt Offering

When a leper recovered from his leprosy, he or she was also required to bring a guilt offering. This may have been because their sickness required a period of isolation, during which time they were unable to meet their obligations to their employer, their family and their God. This was no fault of their own, but during this time, they were unable to meet their obligations or carry out their responsibilities. The guilt offering brought forgiveness for this shortcoming.

There are many lessons we need to learn from the guilt offering. Let me offer three suggestions here in this chapter.

Responsible for our Actions

The first great lesson we need to learn from the guilt offering has to do with responsibility for our actions and words. The Old Testament required that the believer be so responsible for his or her actions that they would restore with interest whatever loss another individual incurred as a result of their behaviour. They saw themselves as guilty before God for any injury their actions brought to another human being. They took their word seriously, and if in any situation, they were unable to be true to that word, they would personally pay for any loss with interest.

The law of the Old Testament required absolute dependability and integrity. Each person took responsibility for their actions or words. It did not matter to these individuals if the loss incurred was accidental and unintentional; they still took responsibility and paid back whatever was lost and more.

We have an example of this in Luke 19:

Offerings and Sacrifices of the Old Testament
[8] And Zacchaeus stood and said to the Lord, "Behold, Lord, the half of my goods I give to the poor. And if I have defrauded anyone of anything, I restore it fourfold." (Luke 19)

Zacchaeus was a tax collector who defrauded individuals of their hard-earned cash. When he came to know the Lord, he recognized his guilt and offered to pay back not one-fifth but four times what he took dishonestly from anyone. He took responsibility for His actions. God expects no less of us today.

Are you a person of absolute integrity? Do you give your employer a full day's work for a full day's pay? Do you treat your customers with respect? Do you say things and never get around to doing what you say? Have you been responsible for the loss of another person? The guilt offering of the Old Testament brought these deeds into the open. The Old Testament believer was required to confess these shortcomings before God as sin.

"The Least of These"

Consider the words of the Lord Jesus in Matthew 25:

[41] "Then he will say to those on his left, 'Depart from me, you cursed, into the eternal fire prepared for the devil and his angels. [42] For I was hungry and you gave me no food, I was thirsty and you gave me no drink, [43] I was a stranger and you did not welcome me, naked and you did not clothe me, sick and in prison and you did not visit me.' [44] Then they also will answer, saying, 'Lord, when did we see you hungry or thirsty or a stranger or naked or sick or in prison, and did not minister to you?' [45] Then he will answer them, saying, 'Truly,

The Guilt Offering

I say to you, as you did not do it to one of the least of these,
you did not do it to me.' (Matthew 25)

In this passage, the Lord speaks to individuals who had refused to minister to those who were afflicted and in prison. Jesus accused these individuals of not visiting Him or ministering to Him. He told His listeners that whatever they did not do to others they did not do to Him.

There is a close connection between what we do for others and what we do for the Lord. When we hurt one of the least of His children, we hurt Him. As the writer of Proverbs says:

[31] Whoever oppresses a poor man insults his Maker, but he
who is generous to the needy honours him. (Proverbs 14)

When a person broke faith with another human being, they sinned against the Lord. When someone suffered loss or harm as a result of their actions, they offended their Creator. Not only was the individual compensated for their loss, but they also brought an offering to God for their sin of offending His child.

How important it is that we see this connection between God and His people. If we fail in our duty at work or in the family, we fail in our obligations toward God. We are to do everything for His glory and honour. To fail in obligation toward the least of His children, we fail in our responsibility toward their Creator. God will hold us accountable for this.

No Excuses

Let me suggest one more lesson we can learn from the guilt offering. There were to be no excuses for not making things right. Ignorance was not an excuse. No one can say, "I didn't do it on purpose," or "I didn't know." Whether we know we offended someone or not, if there is an offence, we are to make things right.

History is not an excuse. We cannot say that the offence was a long time ago and at a different time in our lives. Zacchaeus didn't know the Lord when he overcharged his customers, but he chose to make restitution for sins done years before when he came to know Him. The law of the guilt offering stated that even after the offended individual had died, the guilt offering and restitution were still made.

The guilt offering calls us to search our hearts to see if there is any evil way in us. What a different world it would be if those who discovered an offence toward another would go to that brother or sister and make restitution without excuse. How many offences linger in the hallways of our lives? The challenge for us here is to deal with these matters one by one as the Lord reveals them to us. May God give us the grace to make these things right.

For Prayer:

Father, I recognize that I have often sought to excuse my offences. Teach me to take all my shortcomings seriously. I ask that if I have been an offence to anyone, I would have the grace to make things right. I ask for forgiveness for times that I have not taken my responsibilities seriously. I pray that you would teach me to be faithful to my words and obligations. Help me to speak to others as if I were talking to you. Teach me to respect others as I respect you. Give me the grace to walk humbly before my brothers and sisters. May I be a faithful witness to Yu in my words and deeds. May you be honoured in how I live my life and walk with those around me.

Chapter 7 - The Wave Offering

Scattered throughout the Law of Moses are references to what is known as the wave offering. Consider, for example, the instructions of God in Exodus 29:22-24:

> 22 "You shall also take the fat from the ram and the fat tail and the fat that covers the entrails, and the long lobe of the liver and the two kidneys with the fat that is on them, and the right thigh (for it is a ram of ordination), 23 and one loaf of bread and one cake of bread made with oil, and one wafer out of the basket of unleavened bread that is before the LORD. 24 You shall put all these on the palms of Aaron and on the palms of his sons, and wave them for a wave offering before the LORD. (Exodus 29:22-24)

The context of Exodus 29 is the ordination of a priest. Notice what the Lord told Moses to do in these verses. After sacrificing a ram, he removed the fat, the long lobe of the liver, the two kidneys, and the right thigh. Moses placed these in the hands of Aaron and added a loaf of bread, a cake and a wafer. Aaron and his sons then waved the articles before the Lord as a wave offering.

The word "wave" in the Hebrew language means to move back and forth. While it is unclear what the exact movement used was, the idea is that they made a gesture that symbolized presenting these offerings to the Lord.

Exodus 29:26 instructed the priests to wave the breast of a ram offered for the ordination of a priest before the Lord:

26 "You shall take the breast of the ram of Aaron's ordination and wave it for a wave offering before the LORD, and it shall be your portion. (Exodus 29)

In Leviticus 9, Aaron brought a peace offering to the Lord. He burned the fat, the long lobe of the liver and the two kidneys on the altar as required by the Lord (Leviticus 9:18-20). Leviticus 9:21 goes on to say:

21 but the breasts and the right thigh Aaron waved for a wave offering before the LORD, as Moses commanded. (Leviticus 9)

Both the breast and the right thigh were offered as a wave offering before the Lord.

These animal parts, however, were not the only objects waved before the Lord. According to Leviticus 14, the Lord required that the priest wave 1 log of oil (2/3 pint or 0.3 litres) with the lamb offered as a guilt offering:

24 And the priest shall take the lamb of the guilt offering and the log of oil, and the priest shall wave them for a wave offering before the LORD. (Leviticus 14)

At harvest time, Israel brought the first sheaves of grain to the priest who waved them before the Lord:

10 "Speak to the people of Israel and say to them, When you come into the land that I give you and reap its harvest, you shall bring the sheaf of the firstfruits of your harvest to the priest, 11 and he shall wave the sheaf before the LORD, so that you may be accepted. On the day after the Sabbath the priest shall wave it. 12 And on the day when you wave the sheaf, you shall offer a male lamb a year old without blemish as a burnt offering to the LORD. (Leviticus 23)

Consider also the words of Numbers 8:10-11:

10 When you bring the Levites before the LORD, the people of Israel shall lay their hands on the Levites, 11 and Aaron shall offer the Levites before the LORD as a wave offering from the people of Israel, that they may do the service of the LORD. (Numbers 8)

The Levitical priests were offered as a wave offering to the Lord. They were symbolically given to Him but remained to serve the people as His representatives.

Let's consider now what happened to the wave offering after it was waved before the Lord. Leviticus 7:29-34 tells us:

29 "Speak to the people of Israel, saying, Whoever offers the sacrifice of his peace offerings to the LORD shall bring his offering to the LORD from the sacrifice of his peace offerings. 30 His own hands shall bring the LORD's food offerings. He shall bring the fat with the breast, that the breast may be waved as a wave offering before the LORD. 31 The priest shall burn the fat on the altar, but the breast shall be for Aaron and his sons. 32 And the right thigh you shall give to the priest as a contribution from the sacrifice of your peace offerings. 33 Whoever among the sons of Aaron offers the blood of the peace offerings and the fat shall have the right thigh for a portion. 34 For the breast that is waved and the thigh that is contributed I have taken from the people of Israel, out of the sacrifices of their peace offerings, and have given them to

Offerings and Sacrifices of the Old Testament
Aaron the priest and to his sons, as a perpetual due from the
people of Israel. (Leviticus 7)

The breast and the thigh, after being waved before the Lord, were then given to the priest for food. It was a means of supporting the priests as God's representatives.

The wave offering was not always kept. We read in Exodus 29 that the wave offering brought to God for the ordination of the priests was burned on the altar.

22 "You shall also take the fat from the ram and the fat tail and the fat that covers the entrails, and the long lobe of the liver and the two kidneys with the fat that is on them, and the right thigh (for it is a ram of ordination), 23 and one loaf of bread and one cake of bread made with oil, and one wafer out of the basket of unleavened bread that is before the LORD. 24 You shall put all these on the palms of Aaron and on the palms of his sons, and wave them for a wave offering before the LORD. 25 Then you shall take them from their hands and burn them on the altar on top of the burnt offering, as a pleasing aroma before the LORD. It is a food offering to the LORD.
(Exodus 29)

In reality, the Lord told the priests that they were to give everything to Him. They were to keep nothing back.

What does this offering teach us about God and our relationship with Him? One of the things about the wave offering was that by waving it, before God, the people were saying: "God, this offering is yours? It belongs to You. You gave it to me, and I offer it back to You and Your service."

The Wave Offering

The other detail about the wave offering is that while the sacrifice was offered to God in the gesture of waving it before Him, it was often taken back and given to the priest. This taught the people that by giving to God's servants, they were giving to Him. It reminded them of their spiritual responsibility to care for those who represented the Lord and served Him on their behalf. By giving to the priests, they were giving to God.

Some people feel that the only way they can give to the Lord is by putting money in an offering plate at church. A gift given to a brother or sister in need is also given to the Lord. Listen to the words of the writer of Proverbs:

17 Whoever is generous to the poor lends to the LORD, and he will repay him for his deed. (Proverbs 19)

By giving to the poor, we also give to the Lord.

There is another principle we need to see in the wave offering. The law of God stipulated that the breast and right thigh belonged to the priest as his portion. It also required that the priest wave this before the Lord, recognizing that it belonged to Him. He only kept these portions because of the grace of God in providing it for him.

The wave offering showed that everything belongs to God and that it is only because of His grace that we can participate in any blessing. What do we have that has not already come from the Lord? Can we claim any good gift to be truly ours? Can we who know Him claim to be our own? Does not everything belong to Him? Would it not be appropriate as we arise in the morning to lift our hands and say, "Lord, this day and all its blessing belongs to you. You are the rightful owner of every breath I take and

71

every good gift I receive. I offer all I have to you and recognize you as the source of every good I receive this day."

In the course of my ministry, I have had people come to me and express their appreciation for the work I have done. This may be teaching I shared at church, a book I have written, or something I said or did for them. I have always found it difficult to accept praise from people as I realize that were it not for the Lord, I would have nothing of lasting benefit to offer. How do you handle these compliments or expressions of gratitude? I have found this principle of the wave offering to be helpful. When someone praises me for a job well done, I thank them and then find a quiet place where I can literally lift my hands and offer all that praise back to God. "Lord," I say, "all this praise belongs to you. I recognize you as the source of every good I have ever been able to do. I worship you, and thank you that I have had the privilege of being an instrument in your hands for the blessing of your people." I receive the praise and thanks offered but bring it as a wave offering back to God.

The wave offering was a way of recognizing the real source of every blessing and good. It was a physical gesture that reminded the priests and worshippers that all things belonged to God and that they only participated in these blessings because of His good grace and mercy.

For Prayer:

Father, I thank you for the lesson of the wave offering. I recognize that all I am and have belongs to you. Teach me to offer my life, my time and my resources to you as a wave offering. Help me to understand that by giving to others, I am

The Wave Offering

also giving to You. Help me to recognize you as the source of every blessing and good. I ask Lord that I would learn not to credit myself for the successes of ministry and life. Help me to regularly recognize you as the source of every good I have done. May I not keep for myself anything that I have not first entirely offered to You.

Chapter 8 - The Tithe

The tithe is probably one of the best known of all the offerings of the Old Testament as it is often practiced in the church today. In this chapter, I would like to take a moment to consider the law of God concerning the Old Testament tithe. The International Standard Bible Encyclopedia states the following:

> *The custom of giving a 10th part of the products of the land and of the spoils of wars to priests and kings was a very ancient one among most nations. (Orr, James (ed.); Nielsen, John L. (ed.); Mullins, Edgar, Y. (ed.); Evans, Morris O. (ed.). "Tithe," The International Standard Bible Encyclopedia, electronic edition, Laridian, Marion, Iowa)*

What this tells us is that the practice of giving a tithe was not unique to Israel but practiced among many ancient nations.

The first reference to the tithe in the Old Testament is in the book of Genesis.

> *17 After his return from the defeat of Chedorlaomer and the kings who were with him, the king of Sodom went out to meet him at the Valley of Shaveh (that is, the King's Valley). 18 And Melchizedek king of Salem brought out bread and wine. (He was priest of God Most High.) 19 And he blessed him and said, "Blessed be Abram by God Most High, Possessor of heaven and earth; 20 and blessed be God Most High, who has delivered your enemies into your hand!" And Abram gave him a tenth of everything. (Genesis 14)*

What is important for our purposes here is to see that Abraham gave a tenth of the spoils of war to Melchizedek, the king of Salem. Remember here that this incident took place before God revealed His purpose in the law given through Moses.

After deceiving his father and taking his brother's blessing, Jacob fled to Haran to save his life. Tired from the journey, he laid down to sleep at Bethel. As he slept, the Lord God promised to give him that land as his possession. Notice what happened when Jacob woke from his sleep:

20 Then Jacob made a vow, saying, "If God will be with me and will keep me in this way that I go, and will give me bread to eat and clothing to wear, 21 so that I come again to my father's house in peace, then the LORD shall be my God, 22 and this stone, which I have set up for a pillar, shall be God's house. And of all that you give me I will give a full tenth to you."
(Genesis 28)

In light of the promise of God to give him the land, Jacob made a vow to give God a "full tenth" of all God gave him. It appears then that the practice of giving a tenth was established in Israel before the law of Moses.

The first use of the actual word "tithe" occurs in Leviticus 27:

30 "Every tithe of the land, whether of the seed of the land or of the fruit of the trees, is the LORD's; it is holy to the LORD.
(Leviticus 27)

Here in the law of Moses, the Lord claimed a tenth of every seed and fruit of the land. The passage goes on to say that every tenth animal of the flocks also belonged to the Lord:

The Tithe

32 And every tithe of herds and flocks, every tenth animal of all that pass under the herdsman's staff, shall be holy to the LORD. (Leviticus 27)

In Numbers 18, we discover what the people of God were to do with their tithe.

21 "To the Levites I have given every tithe in Israel for an inheritance, in return for their service that they do, their service in the tent of meeting, ... 24 For the tithe of the people of Israel, which they present as a contribution to the LORD, I have given to the Levites for an inheritance. Therefore I have said of them that they shall have no inheritance among the people of Israel." (Numbers 18)

The people of God were to bring a tithe of their animals, fruit and seed to the tabernacle and give it to the priests in return for their spiritual service. Notice the requirement of God for the Levites who received this tithe:

26 "Moreover, you shall speak and say to the Levites, 'When you take from the people of Israel the tithe that I have given you from them for your inheritance, then you shall present a contribution from it to the LORD, a tithe of the tithe. (Numbers 18)

The Levites who received a tithe were in return to offer a tithe of this contribution to the Lord God.

The Law of God required that the tithe be from the best they had:

28 So you shall also present a contribution to the LORD from all your tithes, which you receive from the people of Israel. And from it you shall give the LORD's contribution to Aaron the

77

Offerings and Sacrifices of the Old Testament
priest. 29 Out of all the gifts to you, you shall present every
contribution due to the LORD; from each its best part is to be
dedicated.' (Numbers 18)

It would be easy for the people of God to give what they did not want themselves. This, however, would be an offence to the Lord God.

The prophet Malachi rebuked the priests of his day because they were offering defective animals as their tithe to God. Listen to the words of God to the priests of the day:

6 "A son honors his father, and a servant his master. If then I am a father, where is my honor? And if I am a master, where is my fear? says the LORD of hosts to you, O priests, who despise my name. But you say, 'How have we despised your name?' 7 By offering polluted food upon my altar. But you say, 'How have we polluted you?' By saying that the LORD's table may be despised. 8 When you offer blind animals in sacrifice, is that not evil? And when you offer those that are lame or sick, is that not evil? Present that to your governor; will he accept you or show you favor? says the LORD of hosts. (Malachi 1)

Note also that the person who did not give a tithe was guilty of robbing God. Consider Malachi's rebuke in Malachi 3:

8 Will man rob God? Yet you are robbing me. But you say, 'How have we robbed you?' In your tithes and contributions. 9 You are cursed with a curse, for you are robbing me, the whole nation of you. (Malachi 3)

The words of Malachi 3 are strong. The Lord God cursed anyone who held back his or her tithe.

The Tithe

When Nehemiah arrived in Jerusalem after returning from exile, he surveyed the spiritual conditions of the land. Notice in Nehemiah 13 one of the problems he needed to address among those who had returned from Babylon:

10 I also found out that the portions of the Levites had not been given to them, so that the Levites and the singers, who did the work, had fled each to his field. 11 So I confronted the officials and said, "Why is the house of God forsaken?" And I gathered them together and set them in their stations. 12 Then all Judah brought the tithe of the grain, wine, and oil into the storehouses. 13 And I appointed as treasurers over the storehouses Shelemiah the priest, Zadok the scribe, and Pedaiah of the Levites, and as their assistant Hanan the son of Zaccur, son of Mattaniah, for they were considered reliable, and their duty was to distribute to their brothers. (Nehemiah 13)

The temple of God and His service suffered because the returned exiles were not bringing their tithe. Nehemiah confronted the officials of the land and challenged them to get right with God in this matter. The result was that "Judah brought the tithe of the grain, wine and oil into the storehouses" (Nehemiah 13:12).

The law of God permitted an individual to redeem the tithe. The idea was that while one-tenth belonged to God if, for some reason, an individual needed that tenth for his family, he could buy it from the Lord. In that case, he was to add one-fifth of the value to the object and bring this instead to the priest as his contribution.

Offerings and Sacrifices of the Old Testament
31 If a man wishes to redeem some of his tithe, he shall add a
fifth to it. (Leviticus 27)

While tithes were generally given to support the Levites and their ministry, every third year the Lord commanded His people to give a tithe to help the sojourner, the fatherless and the widow:

28 "At the end of every three years you shall bring out all the tithe of your produce in the same year and lay it up within your towns. 29 And the Levite, because he has no portion or inheritance with you, and the sojourner, the fatherless, and the widow, who are within your towns, shall come and eat and be filled, that the LORD your God may bless you in all the work of your hands that you do. (Deuteronomy 14)

Four New Testament passages speak about the tithe. The first passage is from Hebrews 7:5-10 and recounts the story of how Abraham paid a tithe to Melchizidek.

The next two passages are parallel passages from Matthew 23:23 and Luke 11:42. In these passages, the Lord rebuked the Pharisees and scribes for so diligently tithing everything they had but neglecting matters of justice, mercy and faithfulness.

23 "Woe to you, scribes and Pharisees, hypocrites! For you tithe mint and dill and cumin, and have neglected the weightier matters of the law: justice and mercy and faithfulness. These you ought to have done, without neglecting the others. (Matthew 23)

The final New Testament passage is the story of Jesus about the two men who went to the temple to pray. The first was a Pharisee who prayed:

The Tithe

11 'God, I thank you that I am not like other men, extortioners, unjust, adulterers, or even like this tax collector. 12 I fast twice a week; I give tithes of all that I get.' (Luke 18)

The other man who went to the temple to pray was a tax-collector. He made no mention of tithing or fasting but prayed: 'God, be merciful to me, a sinner!' (Luke 18:13). Jesus concluded His story with the following lesson:

14 I tell you, this man went down to his house justified, rather than the other. For everyone who exalts himself will be humbled, but the one who humbles himself will be exalted."
(Luke 18)

Jesus teaches two lessons about the tithe in these passages. First, the practice of the tithe is a legitimate practice ("these you ought to have done" – Matthew 23:23), but there are "weightier" matters that must never be neglected. These weightier matters are related to justice, mercy and faithfulness.

Second, it is quite possible to give a tenth of all we have to the Lord and still not be right with Him. More important than giving a tithe is the matter of having a right relationship with God. God accepted the tax-collector who did not give a tithe but rejected the Pharisee who boasted of what He gave.

What principles does the practice of the tithe teach us in our present-day? Let me conclude with a few suggestions.

First, the tithe shows us that not everything we possess belongs to us. In the Old Testament, God claimed one-tenth of the crops and herds. If an individual refused to surrender this to the Lord, they were robbing God (Malachi 3:8). The only way the tithe could be claimed was by buying it back from God and adding one-fifth more to its value.

Consider the words of the apostle Paul to the Corinthians in 1 Corinthians 6:

19 Or do you not know that your body is a temple of the Holy Spirit within you, whom you have from God? You are not your own, 20 for you were bought with a price. So glorify God in your body. (1 Corinthians 6)

The apostle tells us that as believers in Jesus Christ, the Holy Spirit has come to live in us. He claims not just ten percent of our body but the whole thing. The body in which we live says Paul, is not our own. The Lord Jesus bought us at the cost of His life. Everything we have is His. The tithe introduced us to this concept.

What is true of our bodies is also true of what we do with our bodies. Speaking about a master who owned a servant Jesus said in Luke 17:

9 Does he thank the servant because he did what was commanded? 10 So you also, when you have done all that you were commanded, say, 'We are unworthy servants; we have only done what was our duty.'" (Luke 17)

We cannot congratulate ourselves for doing what God has told us to do. As servants, we owe this to the Lord to whom our bodies belong. Everything we have we have received from God. What can we claim as ours that we have not received first from God? Our bodies and all we have belong to God.

The second principle the tithe teaches us is that as servants of God, we have an obligation to give the resources God has given us so that His servants and the work of His kingdom will not suffer. The tithe was used principally to support the work of God in the tabernacle. It was the responsibility of God's people to provide all that was necessary so that this work would prosper.

In the book of Haggai, the Lord rebuked His people because they used their resources to panel their houses while the temple was in ruins. The result was that the curse of God fell on them as a nation:

3 Then the word of the LORD came by the hand of Haggai the prophet, 4 "Is it a time for you yourselves to dwell in your panelled houses, while this house lies in ruins? 5 Now, therefore, thus says the LORD of hosts: Consider your ways. 6 You have sown much, and harvested little. You eat, but you never have enough; you drink, but you never have your fill. You clothe yourselves, but no one is warm. And he who earns wages does so to put them into a bag with holes. (Haggai 1)

Their refusal to support the work of God brought God's anger on Israel. There could be no blessing if they refused to stand behind the work of God. The tithe reminds us that we are responsible for using our resources to advance the Kingdom of God.

The third vital principle we learn from the tithe is that the Lord deserves the best we have. When the people of God brought a tenth of what they had to the Lord, they had to bring the best of what they had (Malachi 1:6-8; Numbers 18:28-29). To bring a tenth of what they did not want themselves did not honour the Lord. God's people demonstrated what they felt toward God by what they give.

How important is the work of God to you? Do you surrender the best you have for the work of the Kingdom, or is what you give from what is left over after you have used what you want for yourself?

Finally, the teaching of Jesus about the tithe shows us that the attitude of the heart is of utmost importance. Jesus rebuked the Pharisees and scribes because, although they regularly give of their tithe, their hearts were not right with Him. God is more concerned about the heart than He is for the tithe. We dare not measure our spirituality by whether we give a tithe or not. You may give generously to the work of the kingdom of God but not be in a right relationship with the Saviour.

The apostle Paul challenged the Corinthians to give with a cheerful heart:

7 Each one must give as he has decided in his heart, not reluctantly or under compulsion, for God loves a cheerful giver. 8 And God is able to make all grace abound to you, so that having all sufficiency in all things at all times, you may abound in every good work. (2 Corinthians 9)

While giving a tithe was an obligation for all Old Testament believers, God expected that His people give with a cheerful and worshipful heart—demonstrating their love and devotion to Him.

For Prayer:

Father God, we recognize that all we have belongs to you. Thank you for the principles that the tithe teaches us. Help us to take seriously our obligation to supply the resources necessary for the work of the Kingdom. I pray that we would give the best we have with a cheerful and joyous heart. I ask that we demonstrate the value we place on making your name known by how we give of ourselves and our resources. Teach us what you would have us to give. Show us how we can better equip your servants to minister effectively for the glory of Your holy name.

Chapter 9 - The Freewill Offering

In the last chapter, we examined the tithe. The individual who refused to give this tithe was robbing God of what was rightfully His. The tithe was a required offering. We come now, however, to the freewill offering. Unlike the tithe, this offering was given freely to the Lord as an act of praise or thanksgiving. Israel could bring a variety of objects for a freewill offering.

In Exodus 35, Moses asked the people to bring contributions for the construction of the tabernacle. Listen to the response of the people as recorded in Exodus 35:21-29:

21 And they came, everyone whose heart stirred him, and everyone whose spirit moved him, and brought the LORD's contribution to be used for the tent of meeting, and for all its service, and for the holy garments. 22 So they came, both men and women. All who were of a willing heart brought brooches and earrings and signet rings and armlets, all sorts of gold objects, every man dedicating an offering of gold to the LORD. 23 And every one who possessed blue or purple or scarlet yarns or fine linen or goats' hair or tanned rams' skins or goatskins brought them. 24 Everyone who could make a contribution of silver or bronze brought it as the LORD's contribution. And every one who possessed acacia wood of any use in the work brought it. 25 And every skillful woman spun with her hands, and they all brought what they had spun in blue and purple and scarlet yarns and fine twined linen. 26 All the women whose hearts stirred them to use their skill spun the goats' hair. 27 And the leaders brought onyx stones and stones to be set, for the ephod and for the breastpiece, 28 and spices and oil for the light, and for the anointing oil, and for the fragrant incense. 29 All the men and women, the people of Israel, whose heart moved them to bring anything for the work that the LORD had commanded by Moses to be done brought it as a freewill offering to the LORD. (Exodus 35)

Notice that the kind of offerings the people brought to the Lord in this passage:

1) Jewellery (verse 22)
2) Yarn (verse 23)
3) Goatskins (verse 23)
4) Silver and bronze (verse 24)
5) Time and effort (verses 25,26)
6) Precious stones (verse 27)
7) Spices, oil and incense (verse 28)

Notice, also in Exodus 35 the attitude of those who gave these gifts:

1) "everyone whose heart stirred him" (verse 21)
2) "everyone whose spirit moved him" (verse 21)
3) "all who were of a willing heart" (verse 22)
4) "the women whose hearts stirred them" (verse 26)
5) "all the men and women, the people of Israel, whose heart moved them" (verse 29)

The hearts and spirits of those who brought an offering were moved to do so. They gave freely and with a thankful and willing heart. The people brought so many gifts in those days that Moses had to ask them to stop:

The Freewill Offering

6 So Moses gave command, and word was proclaimed throughout the camp, "Let no man or woman do anything more for the contribution for the sanctuary." So the people were restrained from bringing, 7 for the material they had was sufficient to do all the work, and more. (Exodus 36)

The hearts of the craftsmen who built the tabernacle and its holy articles were also stirred, and they gave their time and skill:

2 And Moses called Bezalel and Oholiab and every craftsman in whose mind the LORD had put skill, everyone whose heart stirred him up to come to do the work. 3 And they received from Moses all the contribution that the people of Israel had brought for doing the work on the sanctuary. They still kept bringing him freewill offerings every morning, (Exodus 36)

King David had a burden to construct a temple for the Lord. He contributed large resources from his wealth for this project. 1 Chronicles 29 tells us that among other things, David contributed 3,000 talents (225,000 lbs or 102,000 kg.) of gold and 7,000 talents (525,000 lbs. or 238,000 kg.) of silver.

3 Moreover, in addition to all that I have provided for the holy house, I have a treasure of my own of gold and silver, and because of my devotion to the house of my God I give it to the house of my God: 4 3,000 talents of gold, of the gold of Ophir, and 7,000 talents of refined silver, for overlaying the walls of the house (1 Chronicles 29)

After setting an example for the people, David then asked for a contribution from the people of Israel:

5 and for all the work to be done by craftsmen, gold for the things of gold and silver for the things of silver. Who then will offer willingly, consecrating himself today to the LORD?" (1 Chronicles 29)

Notice the words of David here – "Who then will offer willingly, consecrating himself today to the LORD?" He expected that these offerings be given from a glad and willing heart to the Lord. The result of this plea was another overwhelming flood of gifts dedicated to the construction of a temple in Jerusalem.

Regulations for the Freewill Offering

While the freewill offering was voluntary, Isreal needed to follow some guidelines. The first requirement for a freewill offering is in Leviticus 22:18-20:

18 "Speak to Aaron and his sons and all the people of Israel and say to them, When any one of the house of Israel or of the sojourners in Israel presents a burnt offering as his offering, for any of their vows or freewill offerings that they offer to the LORD, 19 if it is to be accepted for you it shall be a male without blemish, of the bulls or the sheep or the goats. 20 You shall not offer anything that has a blemish, for it will not be acceptable for you. (Leviticus 22)

When Israel offered an animal as a freewill offering, God required a male bull, sheep or goat without blemish. If the offering had a blemish, God would not accept it. There was an exception to this rule, however:

23 You may present a bull or a lamb that has a part too long or too short for a freewill offering, but for a vow offering it cannot be accepted. (Leviticus 22)

The Freewill Offering

A bull or a lamb that had a leg longer than another was allowed if it was a freewill offering. While the freewill offering offered more flexibility, the giver needed to provide the best he or she had to the Lord.

The second requirement for the freewill offering was that it be brought to the tabernacle:

5 But you shall seek the place that the LORD your God will choose out of all your tribes to put his name and make his habitation there. There you shall go, 6 and there you shall bring your burnt offerings and your sacrifices, your tithes and the contribution that you present, your vow offerings, your freewill offerings, and the firstborn of your herd and of your flock. (Deuteronomy 12)

The priests received these gifts and offered by them to the Lord. They would assure that everything was done as God intended.

The freewill offerings were handed over to the gatekeepers for safekeeping until they could be used as God directed.

14 And Kore the son of Imnah the Levite, keeper of the east gate, was over the freewill offerings to God, to apportion the contribution reserved for the LORD and the most holy offerings. (2Ch 31:14)

Another important requirement for the freewill offering can be found in the words of Amos when he rebuked the people of his day:

5 offer a sacrifice of thanksgiving of that which is leavened, and proclaim freewill offerings, publish them; for so you love to do, O people of Israel!" declares the Lord GOD. (Amos 4)

Offerings and Sacrifices of the Old Testament

Notice what the people of Amos' day were doing. They were offering leavened bread to the Lord and publishing their freewill offerings. The Lord commanded that any bread used in worship was to be free of leaven. God's people were ignoring this.

Notice also that Amos rebuked his people for publishing their freewill offerings. In other words, they were letting everyone know what they were giving. Listen to the words of Jesus in Matthew 6:

2 "Thus, when you give to the needy, sound no trumpet before you, as the hypocrites do in the synagogues and in the streets, that they may be praised by others. Truly, I say to you, they have received their reward. 3 But when you give to the needy, do not let your left hand know what your right hand is doing, 4 so that your giving may be in secret. And your Father who sees in secret will reward you. (Matthew 6)

Jesus challenged His listeners to give with no desire to be noticed. It appears that there were religious people of His day who were giving so that people would praise them for their generosity and spirituality. Jesus told those who gave in this way that people would praise them but the heavenly Father would not receive their gift. Both Amos and the Lord Jesus teach that we are to give our freewill offerings without a desire for personal praise or recognition.

Because the freewill offering was voluntary, individuals could give as they were able. In the case of the tithe, God required ten percent. There was no such requirement for the freewill offering. In the book of Ezra, Israel contributed" according to their ability" for the reconstruction of the city and temple.

The Freewill Offering

68 Some of the heads of families, when they came to the house of the LORD that is in Jerusalem, made freewill offerings for the house of God, to erect it on its site. 69 According to their ability they gave to the treasury of the work 61,000 darics of gold, 5,000 minas of silver, and 100 priests' garments. (Ezra 2)

The tithe was used principally for the support of the priests, the poor and needy. The freewill offering, on the other hand, covered a variety of expenses. It supported the construction of the tabernacle and the temple of David's day. It helped rebuild the city and walls of Jerusalem. In Ezra 7, the freewill offering supplied rams, bulls, lambs, and other supplies for sacrifices used to purify the land and restore the worship of God in Jerusalem:

16 with all the silver and gold that you shall find in the whole province of Babylonia, and with the freewill offerings of the people and the priests, vowed willingly for the house of their God that is in Jerusalem. 17 With this money, then, you shall with all diligence buy bulls, rams, and lambs, with their grain offerings and their drink offerings, and you shall offer them on the altar of the house of your God that is in Jerusalem. 18 Whatever seems good to you and your brothers to do with the rest of the silver and gold, you may do, according to the will of your God. (Ezra 7)

David tells us that he gave his freewill offering to thank the Lord for His goodness in delivering him from his enemies:

6 With a freewill offering I will sacrifice to you; I will give thanks to your name, O LORD, for it is good. 7 For he has delivered me from every trouble, and my eye has looked in triumph on my enemies. (Psalm 54)

What does the freewill offering teach us about God and our relationship with Him? Let me make the following suggestions.

The freewill offering opened the door for the people of God to give a variety of gifts to the Lord. Many of the other offerings were regulated. Only specific animals were acceptable for sacrifices. The Lord determined the quantity of oil, wine and flour brought for these offerings. The freewill offering was quite different. An individual could offer jewellery to be melted down for the work of the temple, or they could provide yarn to be woven into material for the priest's garments. They could also give their time as a gift to the Lord. The Lord accepted all of these offerings as a token of love from His people. God allowed for creativity in the freewill offering. The offerings could be a personal expression of faith and gratitude.

Freewill offerings were spontaneous gifts offered from the heart. The freewill gift was the response of the heart toward God. The giving of the freewill offering was an act of worship on the part of the giver. Israel gave of themselves, their time and resources as a means of demonstrating their gratitude to a loving God and His goodness toward them.

What is crucial for us to remember is that it is not the amount we give but the attitude of the heart that is important. In the passages we have examined, we see the repetition of the phrases, "those whose heart was willing," or "everyone whose spirit was moved." The key here was the attitude of the heart. You can give with many different motivations. Only those who give with a heart that is moved by God or a willing spirit can offer their gifts as an act of worship to God. The apostle Paul encouraged the Corinthians to give without reluctance or compulsion but from a cheerful heart:

The Freewill Offering
7 Each one must give as he has decided in his heart, not reluctantly or under compulsion, for God loves a cheerful giver.
(2 Corinthians 9)

The final lesson we need to see from the freewill offering comes in the words of Amos to his people. In the passage we quoted from Amos 4:5, we discover how the prophet rebuked his people for "proclaiming" freewill offerings and "publishing" them. In other words, people gave to be noticed. They wanted everyone to see what they were giving. When we offer our gifts to be seen by other human beings or to receive praise from them, we take the glory that is due to God for ourselves. We cannot expect to please the Lord if we take the recognition He alone deserves for ourselves. We must learn to give in such a way that God receives the glory.

For Prayer:

Heavenly Father, thank you for the gift of your Son Jesus Christ, who offered Himself freely for us. I ask that you would teach us how to give freely in return. Open our hearts to the needs and opportunities around us. Teach us to give with unselfish motives. May we desire that You receive all the glory for the gifts we offer. May our hearts rejoice in giving. May our gifts be an expression of the depth of gratitude we have toward You for all You have done. We offer ourselves freely with joyful hearts. Use us and all we have as you will for your glory and praise.

Chapter 10 - The Grain Offering of Jealousy

In the final two chapters, I want to examine two situations that required a unique offering. The first of these circumstances is described in Numbers 5:12-14:

> 12 "Speak to the people of Israel, If any man's wife goes astray and breaks faith with him, 13 if a man lies with her sexually, and it is hidden from the eyes of her husband, and she is undetected though she has defiled herself, and there is no witness against her, since she was not taken in the act 14 and if the spirit of jealousy comes over him and he is jealous of his wife who has defiled herself, or if the spirit of jealousy comes over him and he is jealous of his wife, though she has not defiled herself (Numbers 5)

There are two scenarios presented here in these verses. First, we have the case of a wife who has been unfaithful to her husband by having a sexual relationship with another man. The second is the case of a man who suspects his wife of being unfaithful, but this is not the case.

In this situation, the sin of unfaithfulness is hidden, and there is no proof of inappropriate behaviour. The partners involved refuse to admit guilt. The husband, however, has his suspicions, and the relationship between him and his wife is suffering as a result.

The husband's suspicions were enough to require action. If not addressed, these suspicions could lead to further sin. In this case, the law of God required that the suspicious husband bring his wife to the priest. At that time, the husband also brought an offering of barley flour to the Lord.

15 then the man shall bring his wife to the priest and bring the offering required of her, a tenth of an ephah of barley flour. He shall pour no oil on it and put no frankincense on it, for it is a grain offering of jealousy, a grain offering of remembrance, bringing iniquity to remembrance.

Notice that the Lord called this a "grain offering of jealousy."

The priest called the woman to approach him. He put holy water in a clay vessel along with some dust from the temple floor. He placed the grain offering of jealousy in her hands. As the woman held the grain offering of jealousy, the priest brought the mixture of holy water and dust from the temple floor. Leviticus 5:18 calls this the "water of bitterness that brings a curse." The priest then placed the woman under threat of a curse with the following words:

19 … 'If no man has lain with you, and if you have not turned aside to uncleanness while you were under your husband's authority, be free from this water of bitterness that brings the curse. 20 But if you have gone astray, though you are under your husband's authority, and if you have defiled yourself, and some man other than your husband has lain with you, 21 then' (let the priest make the woman take the oath of the curse, and say to the woman) 'the LORD make you a curse and an oath among your people, when the LORD makes your thigh fall away and your body swell. 22 May this water that brings the curse pass into your bowels and make your womb swell and your thigh fall away.' And the woman shall say, 'Amen, Amen.'

After reciting these words, the priest wrote the terms of the curse in a book and washed the ink off into the water (verse 23). He then took the grain offering of jealousy out of the woman's hands and waved it before the Lord burning a memorial portion on the offering. After the offering, the curse was official before the Lord. The woman would then drink the water. If she was guilty, the water would cause her great pain. If she was innocent, the water would not affect her. The husband and wife would accept the result of the test, and the matter was considered resolved.

This grain offering of jealousy was a unique offering for a particular situation. It teaches us two important principles.

The first principle the grain offering of jealousy teaches us is the importance of the family unit in the mind of God. We see here the significance of the relationship between husband and wife. Faithfulness in marriage was essential if the family was to function under the blessing of God. Adultery was punishable by death because it was such a grave offence against God and the family unit. When the family began to break down, it affected society as a whole. When one partner was unfaithful to another, it severed the marriage relationship and damaged the guilty party's relationship with God. God provided a means whereby even the suspicion of unfaithfulness was addressed before it destroyed the family and negatively impacted the community in which they lived.

Offerings and Sacrifices of the Old Testament

The grain offering of jealousy teaches the importance of addressing suspicions and hindrances in marriages. In this case, the husband found himself becoming suspicious of his wife's unfaithfulness. The couple needed to resolve this matter if the relationship was to grow and be healthy.

God provided a way for a husband and wife to deal with their suspicions. It was not the will of God that the husband live in suspicion and mistrust of his wife. Nor was it the purpose of God that the wife hide her sin from her husband. Sin needed to be exposed and addressed if the blessing of God was to remain on the couple.

What are the hindrances in your marriage? What kind of things keep you from experiencing the fullness of God's blessing in your life? Are there sins in word or deed that need to be exposed and over which you need victory? Do you need to confess hidden sins so that the blessing of God can be restored? Is the Spirit of God speaking to you about wrong attitudes? All these things will negatively impact your marriage and family. God wants a healthy marriage for you and your spouse. He wants your relationship to be free from obstacles that hinder you from being one. In the Old Testament, God provided a particular offering to deal with one such barrier to the growth of the couple. If we want to experience the fullness of God's blessing in our families, we must come to Him seeking victory over anything that would keep us apart as a couple.

For Prayer:

The Grain Offering of Jealousy

Father God, thank you for how you provided a means whereby the husband and wife of the Old Testament could resolve this matter of suspicion. I ask that you would help us today to be willing to see the seriousness of distrust and other hindrances in our relationship as a couple. I ask Lord that we would not ignore these issues but be prepared to address them for the good of our marriages. I ask that we would not allow anything to come between us as husband and wife. I pray that we would have healthy marriages where every obstacle is addressed and where we experience the victory of the Lord over every suspicion. May our relationships as husbands and wives impact the lives of our children and our society as a whole. May our marriages reflect the presence of God and testify to His grace and healing.

Chapter 11 - Atonement for an Unsolved Murder

In Deuteronomy 21:1-8, we read about the sacrifice required by God for an unsolved murder. The passage gives us an example of the situation that required such a sacrifice:

1 "If in the land that the LORD your God is giving you to possess someone is found slain, lying in the open country, and it is not known who killed him,

We have, in this instance, the case of an unsolved murder. Notice that the death described in this verse is not from natural causes. The phrase "it is not known who killed him," makes it clear that we are dealing with an individual who has died at the hands of someone else. The passage does not indicate whether the death was the result of an accident or a deliberate act. In either case, the individual who caused the death was hiding and refusing to admit his or her guilt.

When the remains of the victim were discovered, the elders and judges measured the distance to the surrounding cities. When they determined which city was closest to the corpse, the elders of that city sacrificed a heifer to remove guilt from the land. The assumption is that the guilty party may have hidden in that city. In doing so, the guilty person brought guilt upon the city.

The heifer offered for the sacrifice was to be one that had never worked or pulled a yoke. God required that the priest make this sacrifice in a valley with running water. The valley had to be one that had never been ploughed or sown with seed (see Deuteronomy 21:4). Commenting on this, John Gill has this to say about the location chosen for the sacrifice:

"which is neither cared nor sown;" that is, neither ploughed nor sown, but quite an uncultivated place; and this the Jews understand not of what it had been, or then was, but what it should be hereafter; that from henceforward it should never be manured, but lie barren and useless (Gill, John: John Gill's Exposition of the Entire Bible, Laridian: Cedar Rapids, Iowa, 2013)

According to John Gill, the valley in which this sacrifice occurred would never again be sown or ploughed. It would remain a barren place. In reality, the valley was also to be sacrificed as well. It would be known as a barren wasteland from that point forward in remembrance of the murder that had taken place. This sacrificed valley underscored the seriousness of the crime that had taken place in the land.

In that valley, the priests broke the heifer's neck. The elders of the nearest city approached the dead heifer and washed their hands over it. As they did, they made the following declaration:

7... 'Our hands did not shed this blood, nor did our eyes see it shed. 8 Accept atonement, O LORD, for your people Israel, whom you have redeemed, and do not set the guilt of innocent blood in the midst of your people Israel, so that their blood guilt be atoned for.' (Deuteronomy 21)

What is important to note here in these words is that the guilt of innocent blood was "in the midst of" the people. In other words, the land had been defiled and bore the curse of sin. The sacrifice of the heifer covered this guilt and shame. While the identity of the individual was unknown, their crime had stained the land and offended their God.

Consider this for a moment. When this murderer took the life of a brother or sister, he brought sin not only on himself or herself but also on the land. Sin is not just a problem for human beings; it also curses our land. In the book of Genesis, we see that the curse of God fell not only on Adam, Eve, but their descendants, and the world in which they lived. The ground no longer freely produced its crops. Weeds competed with vegetables. Adam tilled the land by the sweat of his brow. Eve gave birth to children in great pain. The curse of sin brought sickness and disease to this earth.

The stench of murder polluted the land and rose as a foul odour to God. He would not pour out the fullness of His blessing on this polluted land. The sin that filled that land removed His favour. A sacrifice was required to remove the guilt and restore blessing. What does this sacrifice teach us about God and His purpose? Let me offer these suggestions:

First, the offering for an unsolved murder shows us that sin does not just affect the individuals who are involved but also that land in which they live. Their sin stains our land. What happens to a society that legalizes killing children in the womb for the sake of convenience? What is the impact on our nation when immorality is without restraint? Consider what God did to Sodom and Gomorrah. God did not just destroy the people who practiced such abominations, but the whole city in which they lived. What happened in the days of Noah when the inhabitants of the earth turned their backs on God? Did God not destroy the earth along with its inhabitants? Scripture tells us that God will destroy this planet on which we live by fire. The stain of sin cannot be removed so that the entire earth will be destroyed. Our sin brings the curse of God not only on ourselves but also on our land.

Consider for a moment how God must see our nations and cities with all their sin. The evil that takes place in the land is an abomination to Him. How incredible is the grace of God that does not lash out in vengeance and fearful anger against the foul odour that rises every day from our cities? Does this not show us how important it is, however, for us to deal with sin in our midst?

The second lesson we need to learn from this sacrifice is that we cannot afford to close our eyes to the sins around us. The body of that victim of human crime lay on the ground in Israel and stained the land. How easy it would be to say, "It wasn't me that did it, so I don't have to be concerned."

Sin like this rotting corpse affects everything around it. I cannot afford to ignore sin. The people who offered the sacrifice for an unsolved murder were not the guilty ones, yet they needed to confess the sin in their land. The rotten apple in the basket needed to be removed before the whole basket was affected.

There is no excuse. We dare not excuse our sinful attitudes or actions but saying, "it wasn't my fault; anyone would have done the same in my situation." Why I fell into sin is not the issue.

Atonement for an Unsolved Murder

The issue is that there is sin in my life. You don't say, "I didn't purposefully choose to get cancer, so I don't have to worry about it." The fact that you have cancer is what is important. If you don't address it, you will lose your life. This is how it is with sin. How it got there is not a critical issue. What is important is that it be addressed, confessed and forgiven.

Sin is the most significant problem we have as human beings. It separates us from God, corrupts our land and removes His blessing. The seriousness of sin is demonstrated by the sacrifice required for an unsolved murder. How much sin stains our land? How much ungodliness do we tolerate in our families? What do we excuse in our personal lives? God is calling us to address these matters. There is forgiveness and cleansing in the person of the Lord Jesus. Like the priests of the nearest city to the murder, however, we must cry out to God for cleansing and forgiveness.

For Prayer:

Father God, we confess you to be a holy God who is free from all sin and evil. We recognize that we are sinful creatures who have turned our backs on you. As we look around us in our land, we see the effects of sin. We recognize that our nation has been corrupted by evil and rebellion against Your Holy Word. We understand that sin separates us from You and Your blessing. We take a moment now to confess the offences of our land. We acknowledge the wickedness around us. We confess the sins of our churches. We admit the sins of our own hearts. We pray Father that you would purge this evil from our midst. Thank you that the ultimate sacrifice has been made for sin in the work of the Lord Jesus. We come now before this sacrifice and confess that it was for our sin that He died. We wash now in the blood of this sacrifice and receive by faith the cleansing that it offers. Heal us, heal our churches, heal our land through the power of Jesus' blood.

Light To My Path Book Distribution

Light To My Path Book Distribution (LTMP) is a book writing and distribution ministry reaching out to needy Christian workers in Asia, Latin America, and Africa. Many Christian workers in developing countries do not have the resources necessary to obtain Bible training or purchase Bible study materials for their ministries and personal encouragement.

F. Wayne Mac Leod is a member of Action International Ministries and has been writing these books with a goal to distribute them freely to needy pastors and Christian workers around the world.

These books are being used in preaching, teaching, evangelism and encouragement of local believers in over sixty countries. Books have now been translated into several languages. The goal is to make them available to as many believers as possible.

The ministry of LTMP is a faith-based ministry, and we trust the Lord for the resources necessary to distribute the books for the encouragement and strengthening of believers around the world. Would you pray that the Lord would open doors for the translation and further distribution of these books? For more information about Light To My Path Book Distribution visit our website at www.lighttomypath.ca

Printed in Great Britain
by Amazon